D1609136

INSTRUCTOR'S MANUAL TO ACCOMPANY

INTRODUCTION TO

OPERATIONS RESEARCH MODELS

LEON COOPER, Ph.D.

School of Engineering
& Applied Science
Southern Methodist University

U. NARAYAN BHAT, Ph.D.

School of Engineering
& Applied Science
Southern Methodist University

LARRY J. LeBLANC, Ph.D.

School of Engineering
& Applied Science
Southern Methodist University

W. B. SAUNDERS COMPANY
Philadelphia, London, Toronto

Contents for Introduction to Operations
Research Models Instructor's Manual

CHAPTER 2

Problem 1

x_1 = acres of green beans

x_2 = acres of soybeans

x_3 = acres of corn

x_4 = acres of lima beans

x_5 = acres of barley

$$\max x_o = (280x_1 + 310x_2 + 90x_3 + 325x_4 + 200x_5)$$
$$- 3(15x_1 + 30x_2 + 5x_3 + 15x_4 + 20x_5)$$
$$- 2(50x_1 + 30x_2 + 10x_3 + 40x_4 + 30x_5)$$
$$- (100x_1 + 90x_2 + 40x_3 + 100x_4 + 50x_5)$$
$$- 50(100 - x_1 - x_2 - x_3 - x_4 - x_5)$$

s.t.: 1) $50x_1 + 30x_2 + 10x_3 + 40x_4 + 30x_5 \leq 1500$

2) $3(15x_1 + 30x_2 + 5x_3 + 15x_4 + 20x_5)$
$$+ 2(50x_1 + 30x_2 + 10x_3 + 40x_4 + 30x_5)$$
$$+ (100x_1 + 90x_2 + 40x_3 + 100x_4 + 50x_5)$$
$$+ 50(100 - (x_1 + x_2 + x_3 + x_4 + x_5)) \leq 15000$$

3) $x_1 + x_2 + x_3 + x_4 + x_5 \quad 100$

$$x_i \geq 0 \text{ for all } i$$

Simplified: $85x_1 + 120x_2 + 65x_3' + 150x_4 + 150x_5 - 5000 = x_o$

s.t.: $50x_1 + 30x_2 + 10x_3 + 40x_4 + 30x_5 \leq 1500$

$195x_1 + 190x_2 + 25x_3 + 175x_4 + 120x_5 \leq 10000$

$x_1 + x_2 + x_3 + x_4 + x_5 \leq 100$

$x_i \geq 0 \text{ for all } i$

Problem 2

x_1 = number of straight back chairs

x_2 = number of lounge chairs

x_3 = number of rocking chairs

$$\max x_o = 20x_1 + 35x_2 + 26x_3$$

s.t.:
$$10x_1 + 15x_2 + 8x_3 \leq 2600$$
$$6x_1 + 10x_2 + 8x_3 \leq 2200$$
$$15x_1 + 25x_2 + 20x_3 \leq 3400$$

$$x_i \geq 0 \text{ for all } i.$$

Problem 3

x_1 = pounds of milk used to make cheese

x_2 = pounds of milk used as milk

x_3 = pounds of milk used to make butter

$$\max x_0 = 6x_1 + 15x_2 + 4x_3$$

s.t.:
$$x_1 + x_2 + x_3 \leq 200,000$$
$$x_1 \geq 25,000$$
$$x_2 \leq 75,000$$
$$x_3 \leq 120,000$$
$$x_4 \leq 45,000$$

$$x_i \geq 0, \ i = 1,2,3.$$

Problem 4

$$x_{ij} = \text{number of technicians from location } i \text{ assigned to customer } j$$

$$\min x_o = 7x_{11} + 8x_{12} + 5x_{13} + 6x_{14} + 4x_{15} + 10x_{21} + 3x_{22} + 6x_{23} + 7x_{24}$$

$$+ 8x_{25} + 7x_{31} + 9x_{32} + 6x_{33} + 5x_{34} + 5x_{35} + 9x_{41} + 8x_{42} + 6x_{43}$$

$$+ 7x_{44} + 7x_{45}$$

s.t.:
$$x_{11} + x_{12} + x_{13} + x_{14} + x_{15} \leq 23$$

$$x_{21} + x_{22} + x_{23} + x_{24} + x_{25} \leq 19$$

$$x_{31} + x_{32} + x_{33} + x_{34} + x_{35} \leq 47$$

$$x_{41} + x_{42} + x_{43} + x_{44} + x_{45} \leq 33$$

$$x_{11} + x_{21} + x_{31} + x_{41} = 18$$

$$x_{12} + x_{22} + x_{32} + x_{42} = 27$$

$$x_{13} + x_{23} + x_{33} + x_{43} = 22$$

$$x_{14} + x_{24} + x_{34} + x_{44} = 37$$

$$x_{15} + x_{25} + x_{35} + x_{45} = 18$$

$$x_{ij} \geq 0; \text{ for all } i \text{ and } j.$$

Problem 5

x_1, x_2, and x_3 = gal. of R. Red, R. Rosi and B.W. respectively

$$\max x_o = 2x_1 + 3x_2 + 5x_3$$

s.t.: $\quad 1.5x_1 + 3.0x_2 + .5x_3 \leq 300$

$\quad\quad 1.1x_1 + 1.5x_2 + 2.8x_3 \leq 325$

$\quad\quad 1.8x_1 + 1.6x_2 + 1.3x_3 \leq 150$

$\quad\quad 1.0x_1 + 1.5x_2 + .5x_3 \leq 220$

$$x_1, x_2, x_3 \geq 0$$

Problem 6

x_1 = daily amount of vanilla

x_2 = daily amount of chocolate

x_3 = daily amount of coffee

x_4 = daily amount of strawberry

x_5 = daily amount of cherry

x_6 = daily amount of banana

x_7 = daily amount of peach

$$\max x_o = .6x_1 + .7x_2 + .65x_3 + .63x_4 + .62x_5 + .71x_6 + .6x_7$$

s.t.: $\quad .62x_1 + .55x_2 + .52x_3 + .6x_4 + .61x_5 + .64x_6 + .56x_7 \leq 500$

$\quad\quad .40x_1 + .50x_2 + .45x_3 + .42x_4 + .43x_5 + .41x_6 + .40x_7 \leq 300$

$\quad\quad .10x_1 + .15x_2 + .13x_3 + .14x_4 + .12x_5 + .13x_6 + .11x_7 \leq 2000$

$$x_i \geq 0 \text{ for all } i.$$

Problem 7

x_1 = dollars invested in automobile

x_2 = dollars invested in home mortgage

x_3 = dollars invested in personal

x_4 = dollars invested in miscellaneous

x_5 = dollars invested in banks

$$\max\ x_o = 8x_1 + 9x_2 + 10x_3 + 12x_4 + 9x_5$$

s.t.:

$$x_5 \le .25(x_1 + x_2 + x_3 + x_4 + x_5)$$

$$x_3 \le .10(x_1 + x_2 + x_3 + x_4 + x_5)$$

$$x_2 \le .45(x_1 + x_2 + x_4)$$

$$x_3 \le x_5$$

$$x_1 + x_2 + x_3 + x_4 + x_5 \le 5,000,000$$

$$x_i \ge 0 \text{ for all } i.$$

Problem 8

x_{ij} = number of households of type i contacted during time of day j.

$i = 1$ = children

$i = 2$ = no children

$j = 1$ = day

$j = 2$ = evening

$$\min\ x_o = 25x_{11} + 30x_{12} + 20x_{21} + 24x_{22}$$

s.t.:

$$x_{11} + x_{12} + x_{21} + x_{22} \ge 2000$$

$$x_{11} + x_{12} \ge 700$$

$$x_{21} + x_{22} \ge 350$$

$$x_{11} + x_{21} \le x_{12} + x_{22}$$

$$x_{ij} \ge 0 \text{ all } i \text{ and } j.$$

Problem 9

$$x_1 = \text{units of product A}$$

$$x_2 = \text{units of product B}$$

$$x_3 = \text{units of product C}$$

$$\max x_0 = 3.5x_1 + 5.5x_2 + 4.5x_3$$

s.t.: $40x_1 + 30x_2 + 35x_3 \leq 2880$ min.

$$x_1 \qquad\qquad\qquad \geq 800$$

$$x_2 \qquad\qquad \geq 350$$

$$x_3 \geq 350$$

$$x_i \geq 0 \text{ all } i.$$

Problem 10

$$x_i = \text{amount of work time for inspector i.}$$

$$\min x_0 = 3.75x_1 + 3.10x_2 + 3.50x_2$$

s.t.: $x_1 \qquad\qquad \leq 5$

$$x_2 \qquad \leq 5$$

$$x_3 \leq 5$$

$$.97(320x_1) + .98(230)x_2 + .95(350)x_3 \geq 2200(.98)$$

$$x_1, x_2, x_3 \geq 0$$

Problem 11

$$x_i = \text{amount of fuel i.}$$

$$\min z = 5x_1 + 6x_2 + 4x_3$$

$$\text{s.t.:} \quad 4x_1 + 4.5x_2 + 3.5x_3 \leq 50$$

$$x_1 + 0x_2 + 2x_3 \leq 20$$

$$x_1 \leq 10$$

$$x_2 \leq 5$$

$$x_3 \leq 15$$

$$x_i \geq 0; \; i = 1,2,3$$

Problem 12

$$x_{ij} = \text{amount produced in period i, in time type;}$$

$$I_i = \text{inventory at end of period i}$$

$$\min x_o = 4.8(x_{11} + x_{21} + x_{31}) + 6.0(x_{12} + x_{22} + x_{32})$$

$$+ 2.4(I_1 + I_2)$$

$$x_{11} + x_{21} + x_{31} \leq 1920$$

$$x_{12} + x_{22} + x_{43} \leq 1320$$

$$x_{11} + x_{12} - I_1 = 1200$$

$$x_{21} + x_{22} + I_1 - I_2 = 3600$$

$$x_{31} + x_{32} + I_2 = 2400$$

Problem 13

Let x_{ij} = amount of order j for press i.

$$\min x_o = 3.40x_{11} + 3.80x_{12} + 3.20x_{13} + 2.90x_{14} + 3.10x_{15} + 2.80x_{21}$$

$$+ 3.25x_{22} + 3.35x_{23} + 2.50x_{24} + 3.40x_{25} + 2.40x_{31} + 2.50x_{32}$$

let x_{ij} = amount of order i for press j

$$x_{11} + x_{21} + x_{31} + x_{41} + x_{51} \leq 60,000$$

$$x_{12} + x_{22} + x_{32} + x_{42} + x_{52} \leq 80,000$$

$$x_{13} + x_{23} + x_{33} + x_{43} + x_{53} \leq 50,000$$

$$x_{11} + x_{12} + x_{13} = 12,000$$

$$x_{21} + x_{22} + x_{23} = 18,000$$

$$x_{31} + x_{32} + x_{33} = 25,000$$

$$x_{41} + x_{42} + x_{43} = 30,000$$

$$x_{51} + x_{52} + x_{53} = 20,000$$

$$x_{ij} \geq 0 \text{ for all i and j.}$$

Problem 14

4 refineries: $i = 1 \to 3$

7 marketing areas: $j = 1 \to 7$

let x_{ij} = amount of gas produced at refinery i shipped to market j

max profit = x_o = $x_{11}(.25-.15-.06) + x_{21}(.25-.12-.03) +$

$+ x_{31}(.25-.13-.04) + x_{41}(.25-.14-.07) + x_{12}(.23-.15-.05)$

$+ x_{22}(.23-.12-.07) + x_{32}(.23-.13-.08) + x_{42}(.23-.14-.04)$

$+ x_{13}(.21-.15-.02) + x_{23}(.21-.12-.05) + x_{33}(.21-.13-.06)$

$+ x_{43}(.21-.14-.04) + x_{14}(.24-.15-.06) + x_{24}(.24-.12-.08)$

$+ x_{34}(.24-.13-.05) + x_{44}(.24-.14-.07) + x_{15}(.20-.15-.03)$

$+ x_{25}(.20-.12-.06) + x_{35}(.20-.13-.05) + x_{45}(.20-.14-.04)$

$+ x_{16}(.22-.15-.06) + x_{26}(.22-.12-.09) + x_{36}(.22-.13-.08)$

$+ x_{46}(.22-.14-.07) + x_{17}(.23-.15-.03) + x_{27}(.23-.12-.02)$

$+ x_{37}(.23-.13-.05) + x_{47}(.23-.14-.04).$

s.t.: $x_{11} + x_{12} + x_{13} + x_{14} + x_{15} + x_{16} + x_{17} \le 350,000$

$x_{21} + x_{22} + x_{23} + x_{24} + x_{25} + x_{26} + x_{27} \le 250,000$

$x_{31} + x_{32} + x_{33} + x_{34} + x_{35} + x_{36} + x_{37} \le 150,000$

$x_{41} + x_{42} + x_{43} + x_{44} + x_{45} + x_{46} + x_{47} \le 400,000$

$x_{11} + x_{21} + x_{31} + x_{41} \le 250,000$

$x_{12} + x_{22} + x_{32} + x_{42} \le 300,000$

$x_{13} + x_{23} + x_{33} + x_{43} \le 150,000$

$$x_{14} + x_{24} + x_{34} + x_{44} \leq 350,000$$

$$x_{15} + x_{25} + x_{35} + x_{45} \leq 100,000$$

$$x_{16} + x_{26} + x_{36} + x_{46} \leq 200,000$$

$$x_{17} + x_{27} + x_{37} + x_{47} \leq 150,000$$

$$x_{ij} \geq 0 \text{ for all i and j.}$$

Problem 15

x_{1j} = number of boards from lot 1 cut into pattern j (j = 1,2,3,4)

x_{2j} = number of boards from lot 2 cut into pattern j (j = 1,2,3)

x_{11}	x_{12}	x_{13}	x_{14}	x_{21}	x_{22}	x_{23}
3	2	1	0	2	1	0
0	1	3	5	0	1	3

y = number of complete 3-piece units produced

$$\max y$$

subject to:

$$3x_{11} + 2x_{12} + x_{13} + 2x_{21} + x_{22} \geq 2y$$

$$x_{12} + 3x_{13} + 5x_{14} + x_{22} + 3x_{23} \geq y$$

$$x_{ij}, y \geq 0$$

Problem 16

let x_{ij} = amount of time secretary j spends with millionaire i.

$$\max x_o = 3x_{11} + 2x_{12} + x_{13} + 6x_{21} + 5x_{22} + 3x_{23} + x_{31} + 3x_{32} + 5x_{33}$$

$$\text{s.t.:} \quad x_{11} + x_{21} + x_{21} \leq 1$$

$$x_{12} + x_{22} + x_{32} \leq 1$$

$$x_{13} + x_{23} + x_{33} \leq 1$$

$$x_{11} + x_{12} + x_{13} \leq 1$$

$$x_{21} + x_{22} + x_{23} \leq 1$$

$$x_{31} + x_{32} + x_{33} \leq 1$$

$$x_{ij} \geq 0$$

Problem 17

Let x_{ij} = number of calculators of type i produced in department j.

$$\max x_o = 25(x_{11}+x_{12}+x_{13}+x_{14}+x_{15}) + 20(x_{21}+x_{22}+x_{23}+x_{24}+x_{25})$$

$$+ 17(x_{31}+x_{32}+x_{33}+x_{34}+x_{35}) + 11(x_{41}+x_{42}+x_{43}+x_{44}+x_{45})$$

$$\text{s.t.:} \quad x_{11} + x_{12} + x_{13} + x_{14} + x_{15} \leq 1,400$$

$$x_{21} + x_{22} + x_{23} + x_{24} + x_{25} \geq 300$$

$$x_{21} + x_{22} + x_{23} + x_{24} + x_{25} \leq 800$$

$$x_{31} + x_{32} + x_{33} + x_{34} + x_{35} \leq 8,000$$

$$x_{41} + x_{42} + x_{43} + x_{44} + x_{45} \geq 700$$

$$5x_{11} + 7x_{21} + 6x_{31} + 5x_{41} \leq 18,000$$

$$6x_{12} + 3x_{32} + 3x_{42} \leq 15,000$$

$$4x_{13} + 3x_{23} \leq 14,000$$

$$3x_{14} + 2x_{24} + 4x_{34} + 2x_{44} \leq 12,000$$

$$2x_{15} + 4x_{25} + 5x_{35} \leq 10,000$$

$$x_{ij} \geq 0 \text{ for all i and j.}$$

CHAPTER 3

Problem 1

$$\max z = 4x_1 + 2x_2 + x_3$$

s.t.: 1) $5x_1 + 3x_2 + 6x_3 \leq 38$

2) $2x_1 + x_2 + 3x_3 \leq 18$

3) $x_1 + 4x_2 + 4x_3 \leq 24$

4) $x_1 \geq 0$

5) $x_2 \geq 0$

6) $x_3 \geq 0$

Combination	x_1	x_2	x_3	No solution	z
123	16/13	10/13	64/13	yes	148/13
124	0	2	16/3	yes	28/3
125	2	0	14/3	yes	38/3
126	16	−14	0	no	−
134	0	−2/3	20/3	no	−
135	4/7	0	41/7	no	−
136	−	−	−	no solution	−
145	0	0	38/6	no	−
146	0	38/3	0	no	−
156	38/5	0	0	yes	152/5
234	0	0	6	yes	6
235	0	0	6	yes	6
236	48/7	30/7	0	no	−
245	0	0	6	yes	6
246	0	18	0	no	−
256	9	0	0	no	−
345	0	0	6	yes	6
346	0	6	0	yes	12
356	24	0	0	no	−
456	0	0	0	yes	0

Problem 2

	x_1	x_2	x_3	x_4	x_5	x_6	
x_4	5.0	3.0	6.0	1.0	0.0	0.0	38.0
x_5	2.0	1.0	3.0	0.0	1.0	0.0	18.0
x_6	1.0	4.0	4.0	0.0	0.0	1.0	24.0
	-4	-2	-1	0	0	0	0

	x_1	x_2	x_3	x_4	x_5	x_6	
x_1	1.0	.6	1.2	.2	0.0	0.0	7.6
x_5	0.0	-.2	.6	-.4	1.0	0.0	2.8
x_6	0.0	3.4	2.8	-.2	0.0	1.0	16.4
	0	.4	3.8	.8	0	0	30.4

Solution: $x_1 = 7.6$

$x_5 = 2.8$

$x_6 = 16.4$

$z = 30.4$

all other variables = 0

Problem 3

	x_1	x_2	x_3	x_4	x_5	x_6	x_7	
x_5	1.0	1.0	1.0	1.0	1.0	0.0	0.0	12.0
x_6	0.0	2.0	-1.0	0.0	0.0	1.0	0.0	6.0
x_7	2.0	-1.0	0.0	-1.0	0.0	0.0	1.0	3.0
	-2.0	1.0	0.0	-1.0	0.0	0.0	0.0	0

	x_1	x_2	x_3	x_4	x_5	x_6	x_7	
x_5	0.0	1.5	1.0	1.5	1.0	0.0	-.5	10.5
x_6	0.0	2.0	-1.0	0.0	0.0	1.0	0.0	6.0
x_1	1.0	-.5	0.0	-.5	0.0	0.0	.5	1.5
	0.0	0.0	0.0	-2.0	0.0	0.0	1.0	3.0

Problem 3 (continued)

	x_1	x_2	x_3	x_4	x_5	x_6	x_7	
x_4	0.0	1.0	.6667	1.0	.6667	0.0	-.3333	7.0
x_6	0.0	2.0	-1.0	0.0	0.0	1.0	0.0	6.0
x_1	1.0	0.0	.3333	0.0	.3333	0.0	.3333	5.0
	0.0	2.0	1.3333	0.0	1.3333	0.0	.3333	17.0

$$\text{Solution:} \quad x_4 = 7$$

$$x_6 = 6$$

$$x_1 = 5$$

$$z = 17$$

all other variables = 0

Problem 4

Change to max problem and add slack variables.

$$\max z = -2x_1 - 3x_2 + x_3 + 0x_4 + 0x_5 + 0x_6 + 0x_7$$

$$3x_1 + 2x_2 - 3x_3 + x_4 \qquad\qquad = 8$$

$$x_1 \quad + x_3 \qquad + x_5 \qquad\qquad = 4$$

$$2x_1 + x_2 - 2x_3 \qquad\qquad + x_6 \qquad = 6$$

$$2x_2 + 4x_3 \qquad\qquad\qquad + x_7 = 7$$

$$x_i \geq 0, \text{ all } i.$$

-15-

Problem 4 (continued)

	x_1	x_2	x_3	x_4	x_5	x_6	x_7	
x_4	3.0	2.0	-3.0	1.0	0.0	0.0	0.0	8.0
x_5	1.0	0.0	1.0	0.0	1.0	0.0	0.0	4.0
x_6	2.0	1.0	-2.0	0.0	0.0	1.0	0.0	6.0
x_7	0.0	2.0	4.0	0.0	0.0	0.0	1.0	7.0
	2.0	3.0	-1.0	0.0	0.0	0.0	0.0	0.0

	x_1	x_2	x_3	x_4	x_5	x_6	x_7	x_8
x_4	3.0	3.5	0.0	1.0	0.0	0.0	.75	13.25
x_5	1.0	-.5	0.0	0.0	1.0	0.0	-.25	2.25
x_6	2.0	2.0	0.0	0.0	0.0	1.0	.5	9.5
x_3	0.0	.5	1.0	0.0	0.0	0.0	.25	1.75
	2.0	3.5	0.0	0.0	0.0	0.0	.25	1.75

$$\text{Solution:} \quad x_4 = 13.25$$
$$x_5 = 2.25$$
$$x_6 = 9.5$$
$$x_3 = 1.75$$
$$z = 1.75$$
$$\text{all other variables} = 0$$

Problem 5

	x_1	x_2	x_3	x_4	x_5	x_6	x_7	
x_5	1.0	2.0	1.0	1.0	1.0	0.0	0.0	12.0
x_6	0.0	2.0	-1.0	-1.0	0.0	1.0	0.0	3.0
x_7	0.0	1.0	-2.0	2.0	0.0	0.0	1.0	8.0
	-2.0	-1.0	0.0	0.0	0.0	0.0	0.0	0.0

Problem 5 (continued)

	x_1	x_2	x_3	x_4	x_5	x_6	x_7	
x_1	1.0	2.0	1.0	1.0	1.0	0.0	0.0	12.0
x_6	0.0	2.0	-1.0	-1.0	0.0	1.0	0.0	3.0
x_7	0.0	1.0	-2.0	2.0	0.0	0.0	1.0	8.0
	0.0	3.0	2.0	2.0	2.0	0.0	0.0	24.0

$$\text{Solution:} \quad x_1 = 12.0$$
$$x_6 = 3.0$$
$$x_7 = 8.0$$
$$z = 24.0$$

all other variables = 0

Problem 6

	x_1	x_2	x_3	x_4	x_5	x_6	x_7	
x_5	2.0	1.0	3.0	1.0	1.0	0.0	0.0	18.0
x_6	1.0	2.0	4.0	2.0	0.0	1.0	0.0	26.0
x_7	3.0	2.0	1.0	1.0	0.0	0.0	1.0	30.0
	-3.0	-4.0	-5.0	-1.0	0.0	0.0	0.0	0.0

	x_1	x_2	x_3	x_4	x_5	x_6	x_7	
x_3	.6667	.3333	1.0	.3333	.3333	0.0	0.0	6.0
x_6	-1.6667	.6667	0.0	.6667	-1.3333	1.0	0.0	2.0
x_7	2.3333	1.6667	0.0	.6667	-.3333	0.0	1.0	24.0
	.3333	-2.3333	0.0	.6667	1.6667	0.0	0.0	30.0

	x_1	x_2	x_3	x_4	x_5	x_6	x_7	
x_3	1.5	0.0	1.0	0.0	1.0	-.5	0.0	5.0
x_2	-2.5	1.0	0.0	1.0	-2.0	1.5	0.0	3.0
x_7	6.5	0.0	0.0	-1.0	3.0	-2.5	1.0	19.0
	-5.5	0.0	0.0	3.0	-3.0	3.5	0.0	37.0

Problem 6 (continued)

	x_1	x_2	x_3	x_4	x_5	x_6	x_7	
x_3	0.0	0.0	1.0	.2308	.3077	.0769	-.2308	.6154
x_2	0.0	1.0	0.0	.6154	-.8462	.5385	.3846	10.3077
x_1	1.0	0.0	0.0	-.1538	.4615	-.3846	.1538	2.9231
	0.0	0.0	0.0	2.1538	-.4615	1.3846	.8462	53.0769

	x_1	x_2	x_3	x_4	x_5	x_6	x_7	
x_5	0.0	0.0	3.25	.75	1.0	.25	-.75	2.0
x_2	0.0	1.0	2.75	1.25	0.0	.75	-.25	12.0
x_1	1.0	0.0	-1.5	-.5	0.0	-.5	.5	2.0
	0.0	0.0	1.5	2.5	0.0	1.5	.5	54.0

Solution: x_6 = 2

x_2 = 12

x_1 = 2

z = 54

all other variables = 0

Problem 7

	x_1	x_2	x_3	x_4	x_5	x_6	x_7	x_8	
x_6	50.0	30.0	10.0	40.0	30.0	1.0	0.0	0.0	1500.0
x_7	195.0	190.0	25.0	175.0	120.0	0.0	1.0	0.0	10000.0
8	1.0	1.0	1.0	1.0	1.0	0.0	0.0	1.0	100.0
	-85.0	-120.0	-65.0	-150.0	-150.0	0.0	0.0	0.0	0.0

	x_1	x_2	x_3	x_4	x_5	x_6	x_7	x_8	
x_4	1.25	.75	.25	1.0	.75	.025	0.0	0.0	37.5
x_7	-23.75	58.75	-18.75	0.0	-11.25	-4.375	1.0	0.0	3437.5
x_8	-.25	.25	.75	0.0	.25	-.025	0.0	1.0	62.5
	102.5	-7.5	-27.5	0.0	-37.5	3.75	0.0	0.0	5625.0

	x_1	x_2	x_3	x_4	x_5	x_6	x_7	x_8	
x_5	1.6667	1.0	.3333	1.3333	1.0	.0333	0.0	0.0	50.0
x_7	-5.0	70.0	-15.0	15.0	0.0	-4.0	1.0	0.0	4000.0
x_8	-.6667	0.0	.6667	-.3333	0.0	-.0333	0.0	1.0	50.0
	165.0	30.0	-15.0	50.0	0.0	5.0	0.0	0.0	7500.0

	x_1	x_2	x_3	x_4	x_5	x_6	x_7	x_8	
x_5	2.0	1.0	0.0	1.5	1.0	.05	0.0	-.5	25.0
x_7	-20.0	70.0	0.0	7.5	0.0	-4.75	1.0	22.5	5125.0
x_3	-1.0	0.0	1.0	-.5	0.0	-.05	0.0	1.5	75.0
	150.0	30.0	0.0	42.5	0.0	4.25	0.0	22.5	8625.0

Solution: $x_5 = 25$

$x_7 = 5125$

$x_3 = 75$

$z = 8625 - 500 = 3625$

all other variables = 0

Problem 8

	x_1	x_2	x_3	x_4	x_5	x_6	
x_4	10.0	15.0	8.0	1.0	0.0	0.0	2600.0
x_5	6.0	10.0	8.0	0.0	1.0	0.0	2200.0
x_6	15.0	25.0	20.0	0.0	0.0	1.0	3400.0
	-20.0	-35.0	-26.0	0.0	0.0	0.0	0.0

	x_1	x_2	x_3	x_4	x_5	x_6	
x_4	1.0	0.0	-4.0	1.0	0.0	-.6	560.0
x_5	.0	0.0	0.0	0.0	1.0	-.4	840.0
x_2	.6	1.0	.8	0.0	0.0	.04	136.0
	1.0	0.0	2.0	0.0	0.0	1.4	4760.0

Solution: x_4 = 560

x_5 = 840

x_2 = 136

z = 4760

all other variables = 0

Problem 9

replace x_1 by $(y_1 + 25000) = x_{ij}$; $y_1 \geq 0$

max x_o = $6(25000 + y_1) + 15x_2 + 4x_3$

s.t.: $(25000 + y_1) + x_2 + x_3 \leq 200,000$

$(25000 + y_1) \qquad \leq 45,000$

$x_2 \qquad \leq 75,000$

$x_3 \leq 120,000$

$y_1, x_2, x_3 \leq 0$

Problem 9 (continued)

$$\text{or, max } x_o = 6y_1 + 15x_2 + 4x_3$$

$$\text{s.t.:} \quad y_1 + \quad x_2 + \quad x_3 \leq 175,000$$

$$y_1 \qquad\qquad\qquad \leq \quad 20,000$$

$$x_2 \qquad\qquad \leq \quad 75,000$$

$$x_3 \leq 120,000$$

	x_0	y_1	x_2	x_3	x_4	x_5	x_6	x_7	S
x_0	1	-6	(-15)	-4	0	0	0	0	0
x_4	0	1	1	1	1	0	0	0	175,000
x_5	0	1	0	0	0	1	0	0	20,000
x_6	0	0	[1]	0	0	0	1	0	75,000
x_7	0	0	0	1	0	0	0	1	120,000

	x_0	y_1	x_2	x_3	x_4	x_5	x_6	x_7	S
x_0	1	(-6)	0	-4	0	0	15	0	1,125,000
x_4	0	1	0	1	1	0	-1	0	100,000
x_5	0	1	0	0	0	1	0	0	20,000
x_2	0	0	[1]	0	0	0	1	0	75,000
x_7	0	0	0	1	0	0	0	1	120,000

	x_0	y_1	x_2	x_3	x_4	x_5	x_6	x_7	S
x_0	1	0	0	-4	0	6	15	0	1,245,000
x_4	0	0	0	[1]	1	0	-1	0	80,000
y_1	0	1	0	0	0	1	0	0	20,000
x_2	0	0	1	0	0	0	1	0	75,000
x_7	0	0	0	1	0	0	0	1	120,000

Problem 9 (continued)

	x_0	y_1	x_2	x_3	x_4	x_5	x_6	x_7	S
x_0	1	0	0	0	4	6	11	0	1,565,000
x_3	0	0	0	1	1	0	-1	0	80,000
y_1	0	1	0	0	0	1	0	0	20,000
x_2	0	0	1	0	0	0	1	0	75,000
x_7	0	0	0	0	-1	0	1	1	40,000

$$x_3 = 80,000$$

$$y_1 = 20,000$$

$$x_2 = 75,000$$

$$x_7 = 40,000$$

$$x_o = 1,565,000$$

all other variables = 0

Problem 10

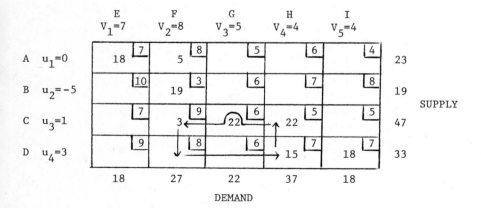

$$u_1 + v_1 = 7$$
$$u_1 + v_2 = 8$$
$$u_2 + v_2 = 3$$
$$u_3 + v_2 = 9$$
$$u_3 + v_3 = 6$$
$$u_3 + v_4 = 5$$
$$u_4 + v_4 = 7$$
$$u_4 + v_5 = 7$$

$t_{13} = c_{13} - u_1 - v_3 = 5 - 0 - 5 = 0$

$t_{14} = \qquad\qquad = 6 - 4 - 4 = 2$

$t_{15} = \qquad\qquad = 4 - 0 - 4 = 0$

$t_{21} = \qquad\qquad = 10 + 5 - 7 = 8$

$t_{23} = \qquad\qquad = 6 + 5 - 5 = 6$

$t_{24} = \qquad\qquad = 7 + 5 - 4 = 7$

$t_{25} = \qquad\qquad = 8 + 5 - 4 = 11$

$t_{31} = \qquad\qquad = 7 - 1 - 7 = -1$

$t_{35} = \qquad\qquad = 5 - 1 - 4 = 0$

$t_{41} = \qquad\qquad = 9 - 3 - 7 = -1$

$t_{42} = 8 - 8 - 3 = \boxed{-3}$

$t_{43} = 6 - 5 - 3 = -2$

Loop for x_{42}

$$\begin{bmatrix} \overset{-}{x_{42}} \to x_{44} \to \overset{+}{x_{34}} \to \overset{-}{x_{32}} \\ \to x_{42} \end{bmatrix}$$

-23-

	$V_1=7$	$V_2=8$	$V_3=8$	$V_4=7$	$V_5=7$	
$u_1=0$	18 ⌐7¬	5 ⌐8¬	⌐5¬	⌐6¬	⌐4¬	23
$u_2=-5$	⌐10¬	19 ⌐3¬	⌐6¬	⌐7¬	⌐8¬	19
$u_3=-2$	⌐7¬	⌐9¬	22 ⌐6¬	25 ⌐5¬	⌐5¬	47
$u_4=0$	⌐9¬	3 ⌐8¬	⌐6¬	12 ⌐7¬	18 ⌐7¬	33
	18	27	22	37	18	122

$$t_{13} = 5 - 8 - 0 = -3$$

$$t_{14} = 6 - 7 - 0 = -1$$

$$t_{15} = 4 - 7 - 0 = \boxed{-3}$$

$$t_{21} = 10 + 5 - 7 = 8$$

$$t_{23} = 6 + 5 - 8 = 3$$

$$t_{24} = 7 + 5 - 7 = 5$$

$$t_{25} = 8 + 5 - 7 = 6$$

$$t_{31} = 7 + 2 - 7 = 2$$

$$t_{32} = 9 + 2 - 8 = 3$$

$$t_{35} = 5 + 2 - 7 = 0$$

$$t_{41} = 9 - 7 - 0 = 2$$

$$t_{43} = 6 - 8 - 0 = -2$$

$$x_{44} = 15$$

$$x_{32} = 3 \leftarrow \text{smallest}$$

$$
\begin{array}{ccccc}
+ & - & + & - & + \\
x_{15} \rightarrow x_{12} \rightarrow x_{41} \rightarrow x_{45} \rightarrow x_{15}
\end{array}
$$

$$x_{12} = 5 \leftarrow \text{smallest}$$

$$x_{45} = 18$$

-24-

	$v_1=7$	$v_2=5$	$v_3=5$	$v_4=4$	$v_5=4$	
$u_1=0$	18 · 7	8	5	6	5 · 4	23
$u_2=-2$	10 · 19	3	6	7	8	19
$u_3=-1$	7	9	6 · 22 → 25	5	5	47
$u_4=3$	9	8 · 8	6 · 2	7 · 13	7	33
	18	27	22	37	18	122

$$t_{12} = 8 - 5 - 0 = 3$$

$$t_{13} = 5 - 5 - 0 = 0$$

$$t_{14} = 6 - 4 - 0 = 2$$

$$t_{21} = 10 + 2 - 5 = 7$$

$$t_{23} = 6 + 2 - 5 = 3$$

$$t_{24} = 7 + 2 - 4 = 5$$

$$t_{25} = 8 + 2 - 4 = 6$$

$$t_{31} = 7 - 7 - 1 = -1$$

$$t_{32} = 9 - 5 - 1 = 3$$

$$t_{35} = 5 - 4 - 1 = 0$$

$$t_{41} = 9 - 7 - 3 = 1$$

$$t_{43} = 6 - 5 - 3 = \boxed{-2}$$

$$
\begin{array}{ccccc}
+ & - & + & - & + \\
x_{43} \to & x_{33} \to & x_{34} \to & x_{44} \to & x_{43}
\end{array}
$$

$$V_1=7 \qquad v_2=5 \qquad v_3=3 \qquad v_4=2 \qquad v_5=4$$

$u_1=0$ 18 .... → 5   23

$u_2=-2$ 19   19

$u_3=3$ 10   37   47

$u_4=3$ 8   12 ←   13   33

18   27   22   37   18   122

$$t_{12} = 8 - 5 - 0 = 3$$
$$t_{13} = 5 - 3 - 0 = 2$$
$$t_{14} = 6 - 2 - 0 = 4$$
$$t_{21} = 10 + 2 - 7 = 5$$
$$t_{23} = 6 + 2 - 3 = 5$$
$$t_{24} = 7 + 2 - 2 = 7$$
$$t_{25} = 8 + 2 - 4 = 6$$
$$t_{31} = 7 - 7 - 3 = \boxed{-3}$$
$$t_{32} = 9 - 5 - 3 = 1$$
$$t_{35} = 5 - 4 - 3 = -2$$
$$t_{41} = 9 - 7 - 3 = -1$$
$$t_{44} = 7 - 3 - 2 = 2$$

$$x_{33} = 22$$
$$x_{44} = 12 \leftarrow$$

$$\begin{array}{ccccccc} + & - & + & - & + & - & + \\ x_{31} & \to x_{11} & \to x_{15} & \to x_{45} & \to x_{43} & \to x_{33} & \to x_{31} \end{array}$$

$$x_{11} = 18$$
$$x_{45} = 13$$
$$x_{33} = 10 \leftarrow$$

-26-

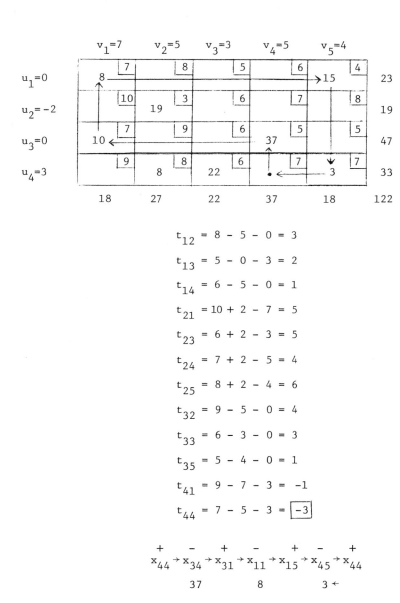

$$t_{12} = 8 - 5 - 0 = 3$$

$$t_{13} = 5 - 0 - 3 = 2$$

$$t_{14} = 6 - 5 - 0 = 1$$

$$t_{21} = 10 + 2 - 7 = 5$$

$$t_{23} = 6 + 2 - 3 = 5$$

$$t_{24} = 7 + 2 - 5 = 4$$

$$t_{25} = 8 + 2 - 4 = 6$$

$$t_{32} = 9 - 5 - 0 = 4$$

$$t_{33} = 6 - 3 - 0 = 3$$

$$t_{35} = 5 - 4 - 0 = 1$$

$$t_{41} = 9 - 7 - 3 = -1$$

$$t_{44} = 7 - 5 - 3 = \boxed{-3}$$

$$
\begin{array}{ccccccc}
+ & - & + & - & + & - & + \\
x_{44} \rightarrow x_{34} \rightarrow x_{31} \rightarrow x_{11} \rightarrow x_{15} \rightarrow x_{45} \rightarrow x_{44} \\
37 & & 8 & & 3 \leftarrow
\end{array}
$$

−27−

Problem 10 (continued)

	$v_1=7$	$v_2=6$	$v_3=4$	$v_4=5$	$v_5=4$	
$u_1=0$	5 ⌐7	⌐8	⌐5	⌐6	18 ⌐4	23
$u_2=-3$	⌐10	19 ⌐3	⌐6	⌐7	⌐8	19
$u_3=0$	13 ⌐7	⌐9	⌐6	34 ⌐5	⌐5	47
$u_4=2$	⌐9	8 ⌐8	22 ⌐6	3 ⌐7	⌐7	33
	18	27	22	37	18	122

$$t_{12} = 8 - 6 - 0 = 2$$

$$t_{13} = 5 - 4 - 0 = 1$$

$$t_{14} = 6 - 5 - 0 = 1$$

$$t_{21} = 10 + 3 - 7 = 6$$

$$t_{23} = 6 + 3 - 4 = 5$$

$$t_{24} = 7 + 3 - 5 = 7$$

$$t_{25} = 8 + 3 - 4 = 7$$

$$t_{32} = 9 - 4 - 0 = 5$$

$$t_{33} = 6 - 4 - 0 = 2$$

$$t_{35} = 5 - 4 - 0 = 1$$

$$t_{41} = 9 - 7 - 2 = 0$$

$$t_{44} = 7 - 4 - 2 = 1$$

$$x_o = (7 \cdot 5)+(4 \cdot 18)+(3 \cdot 19)+(7 \cdot 13)+(5 \cdot 34)+(8 \cdot 8)+(6 \cdot 22)+(3 \cdot 7)$$

$$= 642.$$

Problem 11

	x_1	x_2	x_3	x_4	x_5	x_6	x_7	
x_4	1.5	3.0	.5	1.0	0.0	0.0	0.0	300.0
x_5	1.1	.5	2.8	0.0	1.0	0.0	0.0	325.0
x_6	1.8	1.6	1.3	0.0	0.0	1.0	0.0	150.0
x_7	1.0	1.5	.5	0.0	0.0	0.0	1.0	220.0
	-2.0	-3.0	-5.0	0.0	0.0	0.0	0.0	0.0

	x_1	x_2	x_3	x_4	x_5	x_6	x_7	
x_4	.8077	2.3846	0.0	1.0	0.0	-.3846	0.0	242.3077
x_5	-2.7769	-2.9462	0.0	0.0	1.0	-2.1538	0.0	1.9231
x_3	1.3846	1.2308	1.0	0.0	0.0	.7692	0.0	115.3846
x_7	.3077	.8846	0.0	0.0	0.0	-.3846	1.0	162.3077
	4.9231	3.1538	0.0	0.0	0.0	3.8462	0.0	576.9231

Solution: x_4 = 242.30769

x_5 = 1.92308

x_3 = 115.38462

x_7 = 162.30769

z = 576.9231

all other variables = 0.

Problem 12

	x_1	x_2	x_3	x_4	x_5	x_6	x_7	x_8	x_9	x_{10}	
x_8	.62	.55	.52	.6	.61	.64	.56	1.0	0.0	0.0	500.0000
x_9	.40	.50	.45	.42	.43	.41	.40	0.0	1.0	0.0	300.0000
x_{10}	.10	.15	.13	.14	.12	.13	.11	0.0	0.0	1.0	2000.0000
	-.60	-.70	-.65	-.63	-.62	-.71	-.60	0.0	0.0	0.0	0.0000

	x_1	x_2	x_3	x_4	x_5	x_6	x_7	x_8	x_9	x_{10}	
x_8	-.0044	-.2305	-.1824	-.0556	-.0612	0.0	-.0644	1.0	-1.5610	0.0	31.7073
x_6	.9756	1.2195	1.0976	1.0244	1.0488	1.0	.9756	0.0	2.4390	0.0	731.7073
x_{10}	-.0268	-.0085	-.0127	.0068	-.0163	0.0	-.0168	0.0	-.3171	1.0	1904.8780
	.0927	.1659	.1293	.0973	.1246	0.0	.0927	0.0	1.7317	0.0	519.5122

Solution: x_8 = 31.7073

x_6 = 731.7073

x_{10} = 1904.8780

z = 519.5122

Problem 13

	$V_1=3.4$	$V_2=3.8$	$V_3=3.2$	$V_4=2.9$	$V_5=3.8$	$V_6=.4$	
$u_1=0$	3.4 — 12,000	3.8 — 18,000	3.2 — 25,000	2.9 — 5,000	3.1	0	60,000
$u_2=-.4$	2.8	3.25	3.35	2.5 — 25,000	3.4 — 20,000	0 — 35,000	80,000
$u_3=-.4$	2.4	2.5	3.1	3.3	2.9	0 — 50,000	50,000
	12,000	18,000	25,000	30,000	20,000	85,000	190,000

$$t_{15} = 3.1 - 3.8 - 0 = -.7$$

$$t_{16} = 0 - .4 = -.4$$

$$t_{21} = 2.8 + .4 = 3.4 = -.2$$

$$t_{22} = 3.25 + .4 - 3.8 = -.15$$

$$t_{23} = 3.35 + .4 - 3.2 = .55$$

$$t_{31} = 2.4 + .4 - 3.4 = -.6$$

$$t_{32} = 2.5 + .4 - 3.8 = -.9$$

$$t_{33} = 3.1 + .4 - 3.2 = .3$$

$$t_{34} = 3.3 + .4 - 2.9 = .8$$

$$t_{35} = 2.9 + .4 - 3.8 = -.5$$

$$\overset{+}{x_{32}} \to \overset{-}{x_{12}} \to \overset{+}{x_{14}} \to \overset{-}{x_{24}} \to \overset{+}{x_{26}} \to \overset{-}{x_{36}} \to \overset{+}{x_{32}}$$

	$V_1=3.4$	$V_2=2.9$	$V_3=3.2$	$V_4=2.9$	$V_5=3.8$	$V_6=.4$	
$u_1=0$	3.4 12,000	3.8	3.2 25,000	2.9 23,000 ——→•	3.1	0	60,000
$u_2=-.4$	2.8	3.25	3.35	2.5 7,000← 20,000	3.4	0 53,000	80,000
$u_3=-.4$	2.4	2.5 18,000	3.1	3.3	2.9	0 32,000	50,000
	12,000	18,000	25,000	30,000	20,000	85,000	190,000

$$t_{15} = 3.1 - 3.8 = \boxed{-.7}$$

$$t_{16} = 0 - .4 = -.4$$

$$t_{12} = 3.8 - 2.9 = .9$$

$$t_{21} = 2.8 + .4 - 3.4 = -.2$$

$$t_{22} = 3.25 + .4 - 2.9 = .75$$

$$t_{23} = 3.35 + .4 - 3.2 = .55$$

$$t_{31} = 2.4 + .4 - 3.4 = -.6$$

$$t_{33} = 3.1 + .4 - 3.2 = .3$$

$$t_{34} = 3.3 + .4 - 2.9 = .8$$

$$t_{35} = 2.9 + .4 - 3.8 = -.5$$

$$\overset{+}{x_{15}} \to \overset{-}{x_{25}} \to \overset{+}{x_{24}} \to \overset{-}{x_{14}} \to \overset{+}{x_{15}}$$

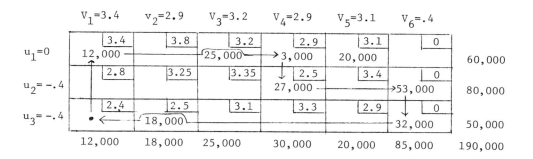

$$t_{12} = 3.8 - 2.9 = .9$$

$$t_{16} = 0 - .4 = -.4$$

$$t_{21} = 2.8 + .4 - 3.4 = -.2$$

$$t_{22} = 3.25 + .4 - 2.9 = .75$$

$$t_{23} = 3.35 + .4 - 3.2 = .55$$

$$t_{25} = 3.4 + .4 - 3.1 = .7$$

$$t_{31} = 2.4 + .4 - 3.4 = \boxed{-.6}$$

$$t_{33} = 3.1 + .4 - 3.2 = .3$$

$$t_{34} = 3.3 + .4 - 2.9 = .8$$

$$t_{35} = 2.9 + .4 - 3.1 = .2$$

$$\overset{+}{x_{31}} \to \overset{-}{x_{11}} \to \overset{+}{x_{14}} \to \overset{-}{x_{24}} \to \overset{+}{x_{26}} \to \overset{-}{x_{36}} \to x_{31}$$

smallest $\to$ 12,000   27,000   32,000

	$v_1=2.8$	$v_2=2.9$	$v_3=3.2$	$v_4=2.9$	$v_5=3.1$	$v_6=.4$	
$u_1=0$	3.4	3.8	3.2	2.9	3.1	0	60,000
			25,000	15,000 — 20,000 → •			
$u_2=-.4$	2.8	3.25	3.35	2.5	3.4	0	80,000
				15,000 ←		65,000	
$u_3=-.4$	2.4	2.5	3.1	3.3	2.9	0	50,000
	12,000	18,000				20,000	
	12,000	18,000	25,000	30,000	20,000	85,000	

$$t_{11} = 3.4 - 2.8 = .6$$

$$t_{12} = 3.8 - 2.9 = .9$$

$$t_{16} = 0 - .4 = \boxed{-.4}$$

$$t_{21} = 2.8 + .4 - 2.8 = .4$$

$$t_{22} = 3.25 + 4 - 2.9 = .75$$

$$t_{23} = 3.35 + .4 - 3.2 = .55$$

$$t_{25} = 3.4 + .4 - 3.1 = .7$$

$$t_{33} = 3.1 + .4 - 3.2 = .3$$

$$t_{34} = 3.3 + .4 - 2.9 = .8$$

$$t_{35} = 2.9 + .4 - 3.1 = .2$$

$$\begin{array}{ccccc} + & - & + & - & \\ x_{16} & \to x_{26} & \to x_{24} & \to x_{14} & \to x_{16} \end{array}$$

65,000   15,000 ← smallest

	v_1=2.4	v_2=2.5	v_3=3.2	v_4=2.5	v_5=3.1	v_6=0	
u_1=0	3.4	3.8	3.2	2.9	3.1	0	60,000
			25,000		20,000 →15,000		
u_2=0	2.8	3.25	3.35	2.5	3.4	0	80,000
				30,000		50,000	
u_3=0	2.4	2.5	3.1	3.3	2.9	0	50,000
	12,000	18,000				20,000	
	12,000	18,000	25,000	30,000	20,000	35,000	190,000

$$t_{11} = 3.4 - 2.4 = 1.0$$

$$t_{12} = 3.8 - 2.5 = 1.3$$

$$t_{14} = 2.9 - 2.5 = .4$$

$$t_{21} = 2.8 - 2.4 = .4$$

$$t_{22} = 3.25 - 2.50 = .75$$

$$t_{23} = 3.35 - 3.20 = .15$$

$$t_{25} = 3.4 - 3.1 = .3$$

$$t_{33} = 3.1 - 3.2 = -.1$$

$$t_{34} = 3.3 - 2.5 = .8$$

$$t_{35} = 2.9 - 3.1 = \boxed{-.2}$$

$$\overset{+}{x_{35}} \to \overset{-}{x_{15}} \to \overset{+}{x_{16}} \to \overset{-}{x_{36}} \to \overset{+}{x_{35}}$$

$$20,000 \qquad 20,000$$

	$v_1=2.4$	$v_2=2.5$	$v_3=3.2$	$v_4=2.5$	$v_5=2.9$	$v_6=0$	
$u_1=0$	3.4	3.8	3.2 / 25,000	2.9	3.1	0 / →35,000	60,000
$u_2=0$	2.8	3.25	3.35	2.5 / 30,000	3.4	0 / 50,000	80,000
$u_3=0$	2.4 / 12,000	2.5 / 18,000	3.1 / ⊗←	3.3	2.9 / 20,000	0 / 0	50,000
	12,000	18,000	25,000	30,000	20,000	85,000	190,000

$$t_{11} = 3.4 - 2.4 = 1.0$$

$$t_{12} = 3.8 - 2.5 = 1.3$$

$$t_{14} = 2.9 - 2.5 = .4$$

$$t_{15} = 3.1 - 2.9 = .2$$

$$t_{21} = 2.8 - 2.4 = .4$$

$$t_{22} = 3.25 - 2.5 = .75$$

$$t_{23} = 3.35 - 3.2 = .15$$

$$t_{25} = 3.4 - 2.9 = .5$$

$$t_{33} = 3.1 - 3.2 = \boxed{-.1}$$

$$t_{34} = 3.3 - 2.5 = .8$$

$$x_{33} \overset{-}{\to} x_{13} \overset{+}{\to} x_{16} \overset{-}{\to} x_{36} \to x_{33}$$

$$25,000 \qquad 0$$

Problem 13 (continued)

	v_1=2.5	v_2=2.6	v_3=3.2	v_4=2.5	v_5=3.0	v_6=0	
u_1=1	3.4	3.8	3.2 25,000	2.9	3.1	0 35,000	60,000
u_2=0	2.8	3.25	3.35	2.5 30,000	3.4	0 50,000	80,000
u_3=-.1	2.4 12,000	2.5 18,000	3.1 0	3.3	2.9 20,000	0	50,000
	12,000	18,000	25,000	30,000	20,000	85,000	190,000

$$t_{11} = 3.4 - 2.5 = .9$$

$$t_{12} = 2.8 - 2.6 = 1.2$$

$$t_{14} = 2.9 - 2.5 = .4$$

$$t_{15} = 3.1 - 3.0 = .1$$

$$t_{21} = 2.8 - 2.5 = .3$$

$$t_{22} = 3.25 - 2.6 = .65$$

$$t_{23} = 3.35 - 3.2 = .15$$

$$t_{25} = 3.4 - 3.0 = .4$$

$$t_{34} = 3.3 + .1 - 2.5 = .9$$

$$t_{36} = 0 + .1 = .1$$

$$286{,}800 = z = (3.2)\ 25{,}000 + 0 \cdot 35{,}000 + 0 \cdot 50{,}000 + (2.5)\ 30{,}000$$

$$+ (2.4)\ 12{,}000 + (2.5)\ 18{,}000 + (2.9)\ 20{,}000$$

	$v_1=3$	$v_2=-2$	$v_3=-4$
$u_1=0$	-3 1	-2	-1
$u_2=-3$	-6 0	-5 1	-3
$u_3=-1$	-1	-3 0	-5 1

$$z = -3 \; -5 \; -5 = -13$$

$$t_{12} = -2 + 2 = 0$$

$$t_{13} = -1 + 4 = 3$$

$$t_{23} = -3 + 3 + 4 = 4$$

$$t_{31} = -1 + 1 + 3 = 3$$

all t's are ≥ 0, so z is optimal

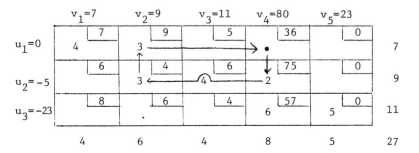

$$t_{13} = 5 - 11 = -6$$

$$t_{14} = 36 - 80 = \boxed{-44}$$

$$t_{15} = 0 - 23 = -23$$

$$t_{21} = 6 + 5 - 7 = 4$$

$$t_{25} = 0 + 5 - 23 = -18$$

$$t_{31} = 8 + 23 - 7 = 24$$

$$t_{32} = 6 + 23 - 9 = 20$$

$$t_{33} = 4 + 23 - 11 = 16$$

$$\overset{+}{x_{14}} \rightarrow \overset{-}{x_{24}} \rightarrow \overset{+}{x_{22}} \rightarrow \overset{-}{x_{12}} \rightarrow x_{14}$$

$$\phantom{x_{14}} \quad 2 \qquad\qquad 3$$

Problem 15 (continued)

	$v_1=7$	$v_2=9$	$v_3=11$	$v_4=36$	$v_5=-21$	
$u_1=0$	7 4	9 1←	5	36 2	0	7
$u_2=-5$	6	4 5 →	6 4	75	0	9
$u_3=21$	8	6	4 →6	57	0 5	11
	4	6	4	8	5	27

$$t_{13} = 5 - 11 = -6$$

$$t_{15} = 0 + 21 = 21$$

$$t_{21} = 6 + 5 - 7 = 4$$

$$t_{24} = 75 + 5 - 36 = 44$$

$$t_{25} = 0 + 21 + 5 = 26$$

$$t_{31} = 8 - 21 - 7 = -21$$

$$t_{32} = 6 - 21 - 9 = -24$$

$$t_{33} = 4 - 21 - 11 = \boxed{-28}$$

$$\overset{+}{x_{33}} \to \overset{-}{x_{34}} \to \overset{+}{x_{14}} \to \overset{-}{x_{12}} \to \overset{+}{x_{22}} \to \overset{-}{x_{23}} \to x_{33}$$

6   ①   4

	$v_1=7$	$v_2=-19$	$v_3=-17$	$v_4=36$	$v_5=-21$	
$u_1=0$	7 / 4	9	5 / →3	36	0	7
$u_2=23$	6 / ←•	4 / 6	6 / 3	75	0	9
$u_3=21$	8	6	4 / 1←	57 / 5	0 / 5	11
	4	6	4	8	5	27

$$t_{12} = 9 + 19 = 28$$

$$t_{13} = 5 + 17 = 22$$

$$t_{15} = 0 + 21 = 21$$

$$t_{21} = 6 = 23 - 7 = \boxed{-24}$$

$$t_{24} = 75 - 23 - 31 = 21$$

$$t_{25} = 0 + 21 - 23 = -2$$

$$t_{31} = 8 - 21 - 7 = -20$$

$$t_{32} = 6 + 19 - 21 = 4$$

$$
\begin{array}{ccccccc}
+ & - & + & - & + & - \\
x_{21} & x_{11} & x_{14} & x_{34} & x_{33} & x_{23} & x_{21}
\end{array}
$$

$$
\begin{array}{ccccccc}
 & & 4 & & 5 & & ③
\end{array}
$$

-41-

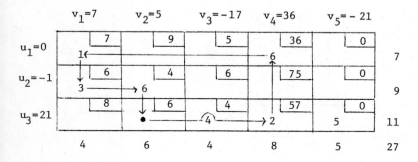

$$t_{12} = 9 - 5 = 4$$

$$t_{13} = 5 + 17 = 22$$

$$t_{15} = 0 + 21 = 21$$

$$t_{23} = 6 + 17 + 1 = 24$$

$$t_{24} = 75 + 1 - 36 = 40$$

$$t_{25} = 0 + 21 + 1 = 22$$

$$t_{31} = 8 - 21 - 7 = -20$$

$$t_{32} = 6 - 5 - 21 = \boxed{-20}$$

$$\begin{array}{ccccccc} + & - & + & - & + & - \\ x_{32} \to x_{34} & \to x_{14} & \to x_{11} & \to x_{21} & \to x_{22} & \to x_{32} \end{array}$$

$$\quad\ 2 \qquad\qquad \textcircled{1} \qquad\quad 6$$

	$v_1=-13$	$v_2=-15$	$v_3=-17$	$v_4=36$	$v_5=-21$	
$u_1=0$	7	9	5	36 / 7	0	7
$u_2=19$	6 / 4	4 / 5	6	75	0	9
$u_3=21$	8	6 / 1	4 / 4	57 / 1	0 / 5	11
	4	6	4	8	5	27

$$t_{11} = 7 + 13 = 20$$

$$t_{12} = 9 + 15 = 24$$

$$t_{13} = 5 + 17 = 22$$

$$t_{15} = 0 + 21 = 21$$

$$t_{23} = 6 + 17 - 19 = 4$$

$$t_{24} = 75 - 36 - 19 = 20$$

$$t_{25} = 0 + 21 - 19 = 2$$

$$t_{13} = 8 + 13 - 21 = 0$$

$$z = 4 \cdot 6 + 5 \cdot 4 + 7 \cdot 36 + 1 \cdot 6 + 4 \cdot 4 + 1 \cdot 57 + 5 \cdot 0 = 375.$$

Problem 16

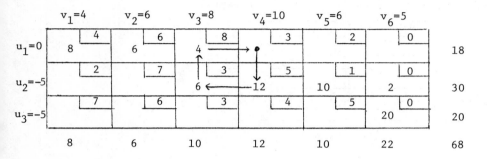

$$t_{14} = 3 - 10 = \boxed{-7}$$

$$t_{15} = 2 - 6 = -4$$

$$t_{16} = 0 - 5 = -5$$

$$t_{21} = 2 + 5 - 4 = 3$$

$$t_{22} = 7 + 5 - 6 = 6$$

$$t_{31} = 7 + 5 - 4 = 8$$

$$t_{32} = 6 + 5 - 6 = 5$$

$$t_{33} = 3 + 5 - 8 = 0$$

$$t_{34} = 4 + 5 - 10 = -1$$

$$t_{35} = 5 + 5 - 6 = 4$$

$$\begin{array}{ccccc} + & - & + & - & \\ x_{14} & \to x_{24} & \to x_{23} & \to x_{13} & \to x_{14} \\ 12 & & \textcircled{4} & & \end{array}$$

$$t_{13} = 8 - 1 = 7$$

$$t_{15} = 2 + 1 = 3$$

$$t_{16} = 0 + 2 = 2$$

$$t_{21} = 2 - 2 - 4 = -4$$

$$t_{22} = 7 - 2 - 6 = -1$$

$$t_{31} = 7 - .4 - 2 = 1$$

$$t_{32} = 6 - 6 - 2 = -2$$

$$t_{33} = 3 - 2 - 1 = 0$$

$$t_{34} = 4 - 3 - 2 = -1$$

$$t_{35} = 5 + 1 - 2 = 4$$

$$\begin{array}{ccccc} + & - & + & - & \\ x_{21} & \to x_{11} & \to x_{14} & \to x_{24} & \to x_{21} \end{array}$$

⑧   8

-45-

	$v_1=4$	$v_2=6$	$v_3=5$	$v_4=3$	$v_5=3$	$v_6=2$	
$u_1=0$	4 0	6 6	8	3 12	2	0 •	18
$u_2=-2$	2 8	7	3 10	5	1 10	0 2	30
$u_3=-2$	7	6	3	4	5	0 20	20
	8	6	10	12	10	22	68

$$t_{13} = 8 - 5 = 3$$

$$t_{15} = 3 - 2 = 1$$

$$t_{16} = 0 - 2 = \boxed{-2}$$

$$t_{22} = 7 + 2 - 6 = 3$$

$$t_{24} = 5 + 2 - 3 = 6$$

$$t_{31} = 7 + 2 - 4 = 5$$

$$t_{32} = 6 + 2 - 6 = 2$$

$$t_{33} = 3 + 2 - 5 = 0$$

$$t_{34} = 4 + 2 - 3 = 4$$

$$t_{35} = 5 + 2 - 3 = 4$$

$$\overset{+}{x_{16}} \to \overset{-}{x_{26}} \to \overset{+}{x_{21}} \to \overset{-}{x_{11}} \to x_{16}$$

$$\quad 2 \qquad\qquad 0$$

	$v_1=2$	$v_2=6$	$v_3=3$	$v_4=3$	$v_5=1$	$v_6=0$	
$u_1=0$	4	6 6	8	3 12	2	0 0	18
$u_2=0$	2 8	7	3 10	5	1 10	0 2	30
$u_3=0$	7	6	3	4	5	0 20	20
	8	6	10	12	10	22	68

$$t_{11} = 4 - 2 = 2$$

$$t_{13} = 8 - 3 = 5$$

$$t_{15} = 2 - 1 = 1$$

$$t_{21} = 7 - 6 = 1$$

$$t_{24} = 5 - 3 = 2$$

$$t_{31} = 7 - 2 = 5$$

$$t_{32} = 6 - 6 = 0$$

$$t_{33} = 3 - 3 = 0$$

$$t_{34} = 4 - 3 = 1$$

$$t_{35} = 5 - 1 = 4$$

$$z = 6 \cdot 6 + 3 \cdot 12 + 8 \cdot 2 + 10 \cdot 3 + 10 \cdot 1 + 2 \cdot 0 + 20 \cdot 0 = 128.$$

CHAPTER 4

Problem 1

$$\max \quad z = 2x_1$$

$$\text{s.t.:} \quad 1) \quad 3x_1 \leq 8$$

$$2) \quad x_1 = \text{integer}$$

By inspection, x_1 can equal any integer from 0 to 2 and still satisfy both constraints.

Given these values, it is obvious that $x_1 = 2$, $z = 4$.

Problem 2

$$\max \quad z = x_1 + 3x_2$$

$$1) \quad x_1 \leq 5$$

$$2) \quad x_2 \leq 3$$

$$3) \quad 2x_1 + 6x_2 \leq 13$$

$$4) \quad x_1, x_2 = \text{integer}$$

Again, by inspection x_2 can be 0, 1, or 2 to satisfy constraints 2, 3, and 4. When $x_2 = 0$, then the maximum value we can choose for x_1 is 5, giving a value for z of 5. When $x_2 = 1$, x_1 can take a value of 3. This gives a value of z of 6. Finally, when x_2 is 2, x_1 can take a value of $0(z = 6)$.

Thus to maximize z, $x_1 = 3$, $x_2 = 1$ or $x_1 = 0$, $x_2 = 2$, in either case, $z = 6$.

Problem 3

x_1 = number of customers reached by television

x_2 = number of customers reached by newspaper

x_3 = number of customers reached by magazine

x_4 = number of customers reached by radio

$$\max z = 400,000x_1 + 200,000x_2 + 250,000x_3 + 100,000x_4$$

s.t.: $400,000x_1 + 150,000x_2 + 200,000x_3 + 100,000x_4 \leq 500,000$

$$x_1, x_2, x_3, x_4 = 0,1$$

Problem 4

Solution	Cost: $	Feasible	Customer Reached
0000	0	yes	0
0001	100,000	yes	100,000
0010	200,000	yes	250,000
0100	150,000	yes	200,000
0011	300,000	yes	350,000
0101	250,000	yes	300,000
0110	350,000	yes	450,000
0111	450,000	yes	550,000 *
1000	400,000	yes	400,000
1001	500,000	yes	500,000
1010	600,000	no	–
1100	550,000	no	–
1110	750,000	no	–
1011	700,000	no	–
1101	650,000	no	–
1111	850,000	no	–

* Optimal Solution is $x_1 = 0$, $x_2 = 1$, $x_3 = 1$, $x_4 = 1$
Optimal Value is 550,000 customers reached.

Problem 5

We let 10,000 represent a very large constant.

$$\max z = 3x_1 + 5x_2 + 6x_3$$

$$\text{s.t.:} \quad 3x_1 + 2x_2 + 4x_3 \leq 11$$

$$7x_1 + 4x_2 + x_3 \leq 12$$

$$-2x_1 - x_2 + 5 \leq 10{,}000 \ (y)$$

$$x_1 + 2x_2 - 6 \leq 10{,}000 \ (1-y)$$

$$x_1, \ x_2, \ x_3 \geq 0$$

$$y = 0 \text{ or } 1$$

Problem 6

Replace x_2 by $x_2 = 2y_2$ where $y_2 = 0,1,2,3,4,\ldots.$

$$\max z = 4x_1 + 18y_2$$

$$\text{s.t.:} \quad 3x_1 + 4y_2 \leq 13$$

$$2x_1 + 2y_2 \leq 1$$

$$x_2 \geq 0$$

$$y_2 = 0,1,2,\ldots$$

Problem 7

Solution	z	Solution	z	Solution	z	Solution	z
(0,0,0)	0	(1,0,0)	10	(2,0,0)	20	(3,0,0)	30
(0,1,0)	4	(1,1,0)	14	(2,0,1)	25		
(0,0,1)	5	(1,0,1)	15				
(0,1,1)	9						
(0,2,0)	8						
(0,0,2)	10						

optimal solution is $x_1 = 3$, $x_2 = x_3 = 0$, $z = 30$

Problem 8

Let x_{ij} = amount shipped from supply point i to demand point j

Let $y_{ij} = \begin{cases} 1 \text{ if point i supplies point j (i.e., if } x_{ij} > 0) \\ 0 \text{ if not} \end{cases}$

$$\min \sum_{i=1}^{5} \sum_{j=1}^{10} c_{ij} x_{ij}$$

s.t. $\displaystyle\sum_{i=1}^{5} x_{ij} = b_j \qquad j = 1,2,\ldots,10$

$\displaystyle\sum_{j-1}^{10} x_{ij} \leq 9, \qquad i = 1,2,\ldots,5$

$\displaystyle\sum_{i=1}^{5} y_{ij} \leq 3 \qquad j = 1,2,\ldots,10$

$\displaystyle\sum_{j=1}^{10} y_{ij} \leq 6 \qquad j = 1,2,\ldots,5$

$x_{ij} \leq L\,y_{ij} \qquad$ where L is a suitably large constant

$x_{ij} \geq 0$

$y_{ij} = 0,1$

Problem 9

$$\max G = 10x_1 + 4x_2 + 5x_3$$

$$\text{s.t.:} \quad 3x_1 + 5x_2 + 4x_3 \le 10$$

$$x_1, \ x_2, \ x_3 \ge 0 \text{ integer}$$

$$g_1(\lambda) = \max_{0 \le x_i \le [\lambda/3]} 10x_1 \ ; \ \lambda = 0, \ 1, \ldots, 10$$

$$= 10[\lambda/3] \ ; \ \lambda = 0 \to 10, \text{ and } x_1^*(\lambda) = [\lambda/10]$$

λ	$g_1(\lambda)$	$x_1^*(\lambda)$
0	0	0
1	0	0
2	0	0
3	10	1
4	10	1
5	10	1
6	20	2
7	20	2
8	20	2
9	30	3
10	30	3

$$g_2(\lambda) = \max_{0 \le x_2 \le [\lambda/5]} \left\{ 4x_2 + g_1(\lambda - 5x_2) \right\}$$

λ	$g_2(\lambda)$	$x_2^*(\lambda)$
0	0	0
1	0	0
2	0	0
3	10	0
4	10	0
5	10	0
6	20	0
7	20	0
8	20	0
9	30	0
10	30	0

Problem 9 (continued)

$$g_3(10) = \max_{0 \le x_3 \le \left[10/4\right]} \left\{5x_3 + g_2(10 - 4x_3)\right\}$$

$x_3^* = 0 : 5(0) + g_2(10) = 30; \ \lambda = 10; \ x_2^* = 0, \ \lambda = 10, \ x_3^* = 3$

$$G = 30$$

$x_3 = 0, \ g_2(10) = 30; \ g_3(10) = 30$

$ = 1, \ g_2(6) + 5 = 25; \ g_3(10) = 25$

$ = 2, \ g_2(2) + 10 = 10; \ g_3(10) = 10$

$x_3 = 0, \ x_2 = 0, \ x_1 = 3, \ z = 30$

Problem 10

$$g_1(\lambda) = \max_{0 \le x_1 \le \left[\lambda/1\right]} 5x_1; \ \lambda = 0 \text{ to } 11.$$

$$= 5\lambda; \ \lambda = 0 \text{ to } 11.$$

λ	$g_1(\lambda)$	$x_1^*(\lambda)$
0	0	0
1	5	1
2	10	2
3	15	3
4	20	4
5	25	5
6	30	6
7	35	7
8	40	8
9	45	9
10	50	10
11	55	11

$$g_2(\lambda) = \max_{0 \le x_2 \le [\lambda/4]} \left\{ 10x_2 + g_1(\lambda = 4x_2) \right\}$$

λ	$g_2(\lambda)$	$x_2^*(\lambda)$
0	0	0
1	5	0
2	10	0
3	15	0
4	20	0
5	25	0
6	30	0
7	35	0
8	40	0
9	45	0
10	50	0
11	55	0

$$g_3(\lambda) = \max_{0 \le x_3 \le [\lambda/5]} \left\{ 3x_3 + g_2(\lambda - 5x_3) \right\}$$

λ	$g_3(\lambda)$	$x_3^*(\lambda)$
0	0	0
1	5	0
2	10	0
3	15	0
4	20	0
5	25	0
6	30	0
7	35	0
8	40	0
9	45	0
10	50	0
11	55	0

$$g_4(11) = \max_{0 \le x_4 \le [11/10]} \left\{ 6x_4 + g_3(11 - 10x_4) \right\}$$

$$x_4 = 0, \ g_3(11) = 55, \ g_4(11) = \boxed{55}$$
$$1, \ g_3(1) + 6 = 11, \ g_4(11) = 11$$
$$z = 55, \ x_4 = 0, \ x_3 = 0, \ x_2 = 0, \ x_1 = 11$$

Problem 11

$$g_1(\lambda) = \min_{x_1 \geq [\lambda/1]} x_1^2$$

λ	$g_1(x_1)$	x_1^*
0	0	0
1	1	1
2	4	2
3	9	3
4	16	4
5	25	5
6	36	6
7	49	7
8	64	8
9	81	9
10	100	10

$$g_2(\lambda) = \min_{x_2 \geq \min\{[\lambda],10\}} \left\{ x_2^2 + g_1(\lambda - x_2)^2 \right\}$$

λ	$g_2(x_2)$	x_2^*
0	0	0
1	1	0
2	2	1
3	5	1,2
4	8	2
5	13	2,3
6	18	3
7	25	3,4
8	32	3
9	41	4,5
10	50	6

$$g_3(\lambda) = \min_{x_3 \geq \min([\lambda],10)} \left\{ x_3^2 + g_2(\lambda - x_3) \right\}$$

Problem 11 (continued)

λ	$g_3(x_3)$	x_3^*
0	0	0
1	1	0,1
2	2	0,1
3	3	1
4	6	1,2
5	9	1,2
6	12	2
7	17	2,3
8	22	2,3
9	27	3
10	34	3,4

$$g_4(10) = \min_{x_4 \geq 0} \left\{ x_4^2 + g_3(10 - x_4) \right\}$$

$x_4 = 2, \; g_3(8) = 22 \; ; \quad g_4(10) = 26$

$x_4 = 3, \; g_3(7) = 17 \; ; \quad g_4(10) = 26$

$x_4 = 3, \; x_3 = 2, \; x_2 = 2, \; x_1 = 3, \; z = 26$

$\qquad\qquad x_3 = 3, \; x_2 = 2, \; x_1 = 2, \; z = 26$

$\qquad\qquad x_3 = 2, \; x_2 = 3, \; x_1 = 2, \; z = 26$

$x_4 = 3, \; x_3 = 2, \; x_2 = 3, \; x_1 = 3, \; z = 26$

$\qquad\qquad x_3 = 3, \; x_2 = 3, \; x_1 = 2, \; z = 26$

$\qquad\qquad\qquad x_2 = 2, \; x_1 = 3, \; z = 26$

Problem 12

Note: This problem was meant to be formulated only and
may not be solvable by students at this level.

Problem 14

$$f_1(x_1) = \max_{y_1 = \left[\frac{x_1}{2}\right]} \{y_1\}$$

$$f_i(x_i) = \max_{0 \le y_i \le \left[\frac{x_i}{a_i}\right]} \{y_i \cdot f_i - 1(x_i - y_i)\} \quad i = 2 \text{ to } 4$$

$$f_1(x_1) = x_1$$

$$y_1 = \left[\frac{x_1}{2}\right]$$

$$f_2(x_2) = \max_{0 \le y_2 \le \left[\frac{x_2}{3}\right]} \{y_2 \cdot f_1(x_2 - 3y_2)\}$$

λ	$f_1(x_1)$	x_1^*
0	0	0
1	0	0
2	1	2
3	1	2
4	2	4
5	2	4
6	3	6
7	3	6
8	4	8
9	4	8
10	5	10
11	5	10

λ	$f_2(x_2)$	x_2^*
0	0	0
1	0	0
2	0	0
3	0	0,1
4	0	0,0
5	1	1
6	1	1
7	2	1
8	2	1,2
9	3	1
10	4	2
11	4	1,2

$$f_3(x_3) = \max_{0 \le y_3 \le \left[\frac{x_3}{1}\right]} \{y_3 \cdot f_2(x_3 - y_3)^2\}$$

	$f_2(x_3)$	x_3^*
0	0	0
1	0	0,1
2	0	0,1,2
3	0	0,1,2,3
4	0	0,1,2,3,4
5	0	0,1,2,3,4,5
6	1	1
7	2	2
8	3	3
9	4	2,4
10	6	3
11	8	4

$$f_4(11) = \max_{0 \le y_4 \le \left[\frac{11}{2}\right]} \{y_4 \cdot f_3(11 - 2y_4)\}$$

y_4	$f_3(11 - 2y_4) =$		$f_y(11) =$
0	$f_3(11 - 0)$	$= 8$	$f_4(11) = 0$
1	$f_3(11 - 2)$	$= 4$	$f_4(11) = 4$
2	$f_3(11 - 4)$	$= 2$	$f_4(11) = 4$
3	$f_3(11 - 6)$	$= 0$	$f_4(11) = 0$
4	$f_3(11 - 8)$	$= 0$	$f_4(11) = 0$
5	$f_3(11 - 10)$	$= 0$	$f_4(11) = 0$

$$y_4 = 2, \ y_3 = 2, \ y_2 = 1 \text{ or } 2, \ y_1 = 2$$
$$y_4 = 1, \ y_3 = 1, \ y_2 = 1, \ y_1 = 2$$

The optimal solution is: $y_1 = 2$, $y_2 = 1$, $y_3 = 2$, $y_4 = 2$, $z = 8$. All other possible solutions fail to satisfy the constraint.

Problem 15

$$\text{Max } z = P_1(u_1) + P_2(u_2) + P_3(u_3) + P_4(u_4)$$

$$\text{s.t.: } u_1 + y_2 + u_3 + u_4 \leq 50,000$$

$$u_1 \geq 0, \text{ integer}$$

Problem 16

$$g_1(\lambda) = \max_{0 \leq x_1 \leq \left[\frac{\lambda}{3}\right]} f_1(x_1) = \max_{0 \leq x_1 \leq [\lambda]} \left\{6x_1 - 3x_1^2\right\}; \quad \lambda = 0 \text{ to } 3$$

λ	$g_2(x_1)$	x_1^*
0	0	0
1	3	1
2	3	1
3	3	1

$$g_2(3) = \max_{0 \leq x_2 \leq 3} \left\{(4x_2 - 2x_2^2) + g_1(3 - x_2)\right\}$$

λ	$g_2(x_2)$	x_2^*
3	5	1

$$x_1 = 1, \ x_2 = 1, \ z = 5$$

Problem 17

<u>Problem 17</u>

Assume all 6 will be added.

x_j = number of dealerships going to Division j - 1,2,3

P_j = profit in Division j

$$g_1(\lambda) = \max_{1 \leq x_1 \leq \lambda} P_1(x_1)$$

$P_1(0) = 100$

$P_1(1) = 200$

$P_1(2) = 280$

$P_1(3) = 330$

$P_1(4) = 340$

$$g_2(\lambda) = \max_{1 \leq x_2 \leq \lambda} P_2(x_2 + P_1(\lambda - x_2))$$

$P_2(0) = 200 + 340 = 540$

$P_2(1) = 210 + 330 = 540$

$P_2(2) = 220 + 280 = 500$

$P_2(3) = 225 + 200 = 425$

$P_2(4) = 230 + 100 = 330$

$$g_3(\lambda) = \max_{1 \leq x_2 \leq \lambda} P_3(x_3 + P_2(6 - x_3))$$

$P_3(1) = 160 + 210 + 340 = 710 \ (3,2,1) \ (4,1,1)$

$P_3(2) = 170 + \qquad\qquad = 710 \ (3,1,2)$

$P_3(3) = 180 + \qquad\qquad = 670 \ (2,1,3)$

$P_3(4) = 200 + 210 + 200 = 610$

(4,1,1), or (3,2,1), or (3,1,2);   z = 710

Problem 18

$$\min z = 2x_1 + x_2 + 3x_3 + x_4^2$$

$$\text{s.t.:} \quad x_1^2 + 2x_2 + x_3 + 2x_4 \leq 14$$

$$x_i \geq 0 \text{ integers all } i$$

$$g_1(\lambda) = \min_{0 \leq x_1 \leq \left\lfloor \lambda^{1/2} \right\rfloor} 2x_1 \qquad \lambda = 0 \text{ to } 14$$

λ	$g_1(x_1)$	x_1^*
0	0	0
1	0	0
2	0	0
3	0	0
4	0	0
5	0	0
6	0	0
7	0	0
8	0	0
9	0	0
10	0	0
11	0	0
12	0	0
13	0	0
14	0	0

Similarly, for all x_i; $x_i = 0$ will be the optimal solution.

CHAPTER 5

#1 Let x_{ij} equal the number of units shipped from supply point i to demand point j, where i = 1, 2, 3 and j = 1, 2, 3, 4, 5

Objective Function

Minimize:
$$4x_{11} + 5x_{12} + 3x_{13} + 1x_{14} + 2x_{15}$$
$$+ 6x_{21} + 8x_{22} + 3x_{23} + 4x_{24} + 1x_{25}$$
$$+ 7x_{31} + 2x_{32} + 6x_{33} + 3x_{34} + 8x_{35}$$

Constraints

$$x_{11} + x_{12} + x_{13} + x_{14} + x_{15} = 4$$
$$x_{21} + x_{22} + x_{23} + x_{24} + x_{25} = 6$$
$$x_{31} + x_{32} + x_{33} + x_{34} + x_{35} = 8$$

$$x_{11} + x_{21} + x_{31} = 3$$
$$x_{12} + x_{22} + x_{32} = 2$$
$$x_{13} + x_{23} + x_{33} = 7$$
$$x_{14} + x_{24} + x_{34} = 4$$
$$x_{15} + x_{25} + x_{35} = 2$$

$$x_{ij} = 0, 1, 2, \ldots \quad \text{for } i = 1, 2, 3 \text{ and } j = 1, 2, 3, 4, 5$$

Transportation Network

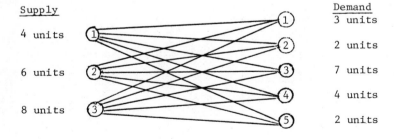

Supply		Demand
		3 units
4 units	①	
		2 units
6 units	②	7 units
		4 units
8 units	③	
		2 units

Let node 6 be the fictitious demand point.

Transportation Network

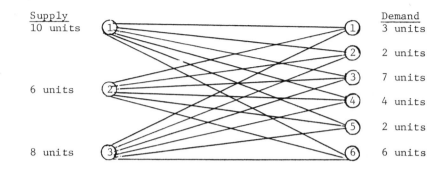

Supplies, Demands and Shipping Costs Table

| | | Destinations | | | | | | |
		1	2	3	4	5	6	Supplies
	1	4	5	3	1	2	2	10
Sources	2	6	8	3	4	1	3	6
	3	7	2	6	3	8	1	8
	Demands	3	2	7	4	2	6	

#3   Let node 4 be the fictitious supply point.

Transportation Network

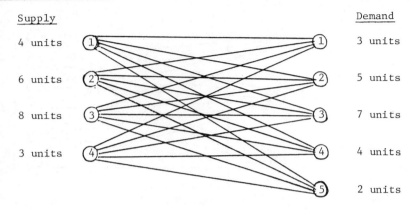

Supply   Demand

4 units   ①   ①   3 units

6 units   ②   ②   5 units

8 units   ③   ③   7 units

3 units   ④   ④   4 units

                                               ⑤   2 units

Supplies, Demands and Shipping Costs Table

		Destinations					
		1	2	3	4	5	Supplies
Sources	1	4	5	3	1	2	4
	2	6	8	3	4	1	6
	3	7	2	6	3	8	8
	4	5	5	5	5	5	3
	Demands	3	5	7	4	2	

-64-

Each node will be broken up so that its capacity is reduced to 1
unit.   The new network would then be as shown below.

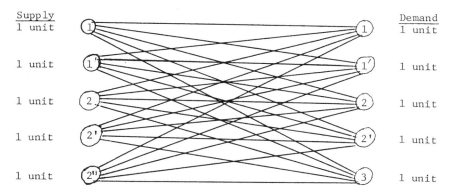

Supply
1 unit

1 unit

1 unit

1 unit

1 unit

Demand
1 unit

1 unit

1 unit

1 unit

1 unit

Shipping Costs

From \ To	1	1'	2	2'	3
1	27	27	13	13	8
1'	27	27	13	13	8
2	16	16	10	10	19
2'	16	16	10	10	19
2"	16	16	10	10	19

An equivalent network with only arc capacities is

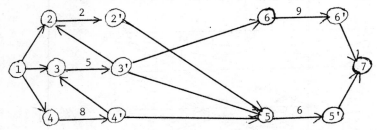

Select the path $1 \to 3 \to 3' \to 6 \to 6' \to 7$ and send 5 units along the path.

Select the path $1 \to 4 \to 4' \to 5 \to 5' \to 7$ and send 6 units along the path.

The maximum flow into node 7 is 11 units.

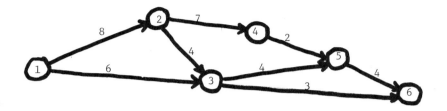

Iteration 1: Select path $1 \to 3 \to 6$ and sent 3 units:

$$x_{13} \to x_{13} + 3 = 0 + 3 = 3$$
$$x_{36} \to x_{36} + 3 = 0 + 3 = 3$$

$$c_{13} \to c_{13} - 3 = 6 - 3 = 3 \qquad\qquad c_{63} \to c_{63} + 3 = 0 + 3 = 3$$
$$c_{36} \to c_{36} - 3 = 3 - 3 = 0 \qquad\qquad c_{31} \to c_{31} + 3 = 0 + 3 = 3$$

The modified network becomes:

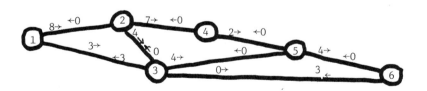

6 continued

Iteration 2: Select the path $1 \to 2 \to 4 \to 5 \to 6$ and send 2 units:

$$x_{12} \to x_{12} + 2 = 0 + 2 = 2$$
$$x_{24} \to x_{24} + 2 = 0 + 2 = 2$$
$$x_{45} \to x_{45} + 2 = 0 + 2 = 2$$
$$x_{56} \to x_{56} + 2 = 0 + 2 = 2$$

$$c_{12} \to c_{12} - 2 = 8 - 2 = 6 \qquad\qquad c_{65} \to c_{65} + 2 = 0 + 2 = 2$$
$$c_{24} \to c_{24} - 2 = 7 - 2 = 5 \qquad\qquad c_{54} \to c_{54} + 2 = 0 + 2 = 2$$
$$c_{45} \to c_{45} - 2 = 2 - 2 = 0 \qquad\qquad c_{42} \to c_{42} + 2 = 0 + 2 = 2$$
$$c_{56} \to c_{56} - 2 = 4 - 2 = 2 \qquad\qquad c_{21} \to c_{21} + 2 = 0 + 2 = 2$$

The modified network becomes:

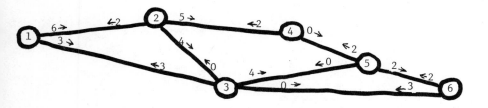

6 continued

Iteration 3: Select the path $1 \to 3 \to 5 \to 6$ and send 2 units:

$$x_{13} \to x_{13} + 2 = 3 + 2 = 5$$
$$x_{35} \to x_{35} + 2 = 0 + 2 = 2$$
$$x_{56} \to x_{56} + 2 = 2 + 2 = 4$$

$$c_{13} \to c_{13} - 2 = 3 - 2 = 1 \qquad\qquad c_{65} \to c_{65} + 2 = 2 + 2 = 4$$
$$c_{35} \to c_{35} - 2 = 4 - 2 = 2 \qquad\qquad c_{53} \to c_{53} + 2 = 0 + 2 = 2$$
$$c_{56} \to c_{56} - 2 = 2 - 2 = 0 \qquad\qquad c_{31} \to c_{31} + 2 = 3 + 2 = 5$$

The modified network becomes:

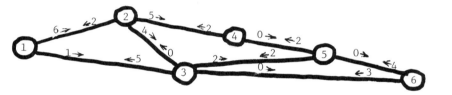

There is no remaining path from the source to the sink with positive capacity, and so the algorithm terminates. The final values are shown below; the maximum flow for node 1 to node 6 is 7 units:

$$x_{12} = 2$$

$$x_{13} = 5$$

$$x_{23} = 0$$

$$x_{24} = 2$$

$$x_{35} = 2$$

$$x_{36} = 3$$

$$x_{45} = 2$$

$$x_{56} = 4$$

The arc lengths are as follows. Note that any arc which does not actually exist in the network has infinite length.

	1	2	3	4	5	6
1	∞	2	3	∞	∞	∞
2	∞	∞	2	3	∞	∞
3	∞	∞	∞	∞	3	5
4	∞	∞	∞	∞	2	∞
5	∞	∞	∞	∞	∞	1
6	∞	∞	∞	∞	∞	∞

Iteration #0
Set $P(1) = 0$
and $T(2) = \infty$, $T(3) = \infty$, $T(4) = \infty$, $T(5) = \infty$, $T(6) = \infty$

Iteration #1
$T(2) = \text{MIN}[T(2), P(1) + b_{12}] = 2$

$T(3) = \text{MIN}[T(3), P(1) + b_{13}] = 3$

$T(4) = \text{MIN}[T(4), P(1) + b_{14}] = \infty$

$T(5) = \text{MIN}[T(5), P(1) + b_{15}] = \infty$

$T(6) = \text{MIN}[T(6), P(1) + b_{16}] = \infty$

Since nodes 2 and 3 received new tentative labels, we set
PRIOR (2) = 1
PRIOR (3) = 1

$\text{MIN}[2,3] = 2$. So node 2 gets a permanent label: $P(2) = 2$.

Iteration #2
$T(3) = \text{MIN}[T(3), P(2) + b_{23}] = \text{MIN}[3, 2 + 2] = 3$

$T(4) = \text{MIN}[T(4), P(2) + b_{24}] = \text{MIN}[\infty, 2 + 3] = 5$

$T(5) = \text{MIN}[T(5), P(2) + b_{25}] = \text{MIN}[\infty, 2 + \infty] = \infty$

$T(6) = \text{MIN}[T(6), P(2) + b_{26}] = \text{MIN}[\infty, 2 + \infty] = \infty$

Since only node 4 had its tentative label changed, we set
PRIOR (4) = 2

$\text{MIN}[3,5] = 3$. So node 3 gets a permanent label: $P(3) = 3$

Iteration #4
$T(4) = \text{MIN}[T(4), P(3) + b_{34}] = \text{MIN}[5, 3 + \infty] = 5$

$T(5) = \text{MIN}[T(5), P(3) + b_{35}] = \text{MIN}[\infty, 3 + 3] = 6$

$T(6) = \text{MIN}[T(6), P(3) + b_{36}] = \text{MIN}[\infty, 3 + 5] = 8$

Since nodes 5 and 6 received new tentative labels, we set
PRIOR (5) = 3
PRIOR (6) = 3

7 (cont)   MIN[5,6,8] = 5.   So node 4 gets a permanent label: P(4) = 5.

Iteration #5
       T(5) = MIN[T(5), P(4) + b$_{45}$] = MIN[6,5 + 2] = 6
       T(6) = MIN[T(6), P(4) + b$_{56}$] = MIN[8,5 + ∞] = 8

       MIN[6,8] = 6.   So node 5 gets a permanent label: P(5) = 6.

Iteration #6
       T(6) = MIN[T(6), P(5) + b$_{56}$] = MIN[8,6 + 1] = 7

Since node 6 received a new tentative label, we set
       PRIOR (6) = 5

       Also, P(6) = 7

Since node 6 is permanently labelled, we are done. PRIOR (6) = 5,
PRIOR (5) = 3 and PRIOR (3) = 1 and so the shortest path is
1 → 3 → 5 → 6 with a total distance of 7 units.

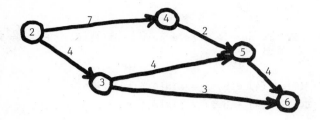

<u>Iteration 1</u>: Select the path $2 \to 4 \to 5 \to 6$ and send 2 units:

$$x_{24} \to x_{24} + 2 = 0 + 2 = 2$$
$$x_{45} \to x_{45} + 2 = 0 + 2 = 2$$
$$x_{56} \to x_{56} + 2 = 0 + 2 = 2$$

$c_{24} \to c_{24} - 2 = 7 - 2 = 5$ $\qquad\qquad$ $c_{65} \to c_{65} + 2 = 0 + 2 = 2$

$c_{45} \to c_{45} - 2 = 2 - 2 = 0$ $\qquad\qquad$ $c_{54} \to c_{54} + 2 = 0 + 2 = 2$

$c_{56} \to c_{56} - 2 = 4 - 2 = 2$ $\qquad\qquad$ $c_{42} \to c_{42} + 2 = 0 + 2 = 2$

The modified network becomes:

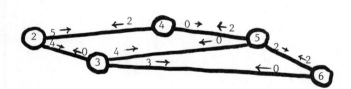

8 continued

Iteration 2:   Select the path $2 \rightarrow 3 \rightarrow 6$ and send 3 units

$$x_{23} \rightarrow x_{23} + 3 = 0 + 3 = 3$$
$$x_{36} \rightarrow x_{36} + 3 = 0 + 3 = 3$$

$$c_{23} \rightarrow c_{23} - 3 = 4 - 3 = 1 \qquad\qquad c_{63} \rightarrow c_{63} + 3 = 0 + 3 = 3$$
$$c_{36} \rightarrow c_{36} - 3 = 3 - 3 = 0 \qquad\qquad c_{32} \rightarrow c_{32} + 3 = 0 + 3 = 3$$

The modified network becomes:

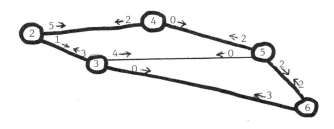

Iteration 3:   Select the path $2 \rightarrow 3 \rightarrow 5 \rightarrow 6$ and send 1 unit:

$$x_{23} \rightarrow x_{23} + 1 = 3 + 1 = 4$$
$$x_{35} \rightarrow x_{35} + 1 = 0 + 1 = 1$$
$$x_{56} \rightarrow x_{56} + 1 = 2 + 1 = 3$$

$$c_{23} \rightarrow c_{23} - 1 = 1 - 1 = 0 \qquad\qquad c_{65} \rightarrow c_{65} + 1 = 2 + 1 = 3$$
$$c_{35} \rightarrow c_{35} - 1 = 4 - 1 = 3 \qquad\qquad c_{53} \rightarrow c_{53} + 1 = 0 + 1 = 1$$
$$c_{56} \rightarrow c_{56} - 1 = 2 - 1 = 1 \qquad\qquad c_{32} \rightarrow c_{32} + 1 = 3 + 1 = 4$$

The modified network becomes:

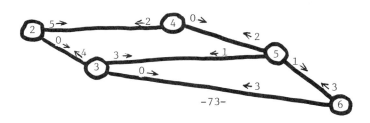

8 continued

There is no remaining path from the source to the sink with positive capacity, and so the algorithm terminates.

The final values are shown below; the maximum flow from node 2 to node 6 is 6 units.

$$x_{23} = 4$$
$$x_{24} = 2$$
$$x_{35} = 1$$
$$x_{36} = 3$$
$$x_{45} = 2$$
$$x_{56} = 3$$

Dijkstra's algorithm is used to solve the problem. A dummy node 6 is used and the distance for each arc is tabulated as shown below.

	1	2	3	4	5	6
1	∞	280	410	600	870	1260
2	∞	∞	290	420	610	880
3	∞	∞	∞	310	440	630
4	∞	∞	∞	∞	320	450
5	∞	∞	∞	∞	∞	340
6	∞	∞	∞	∞	∞	∞

Let $P(1) = 0$, $T(2) = \infty$, $T(3) = \infty$, $T(4) = \infty$, $T(5) = \infty$, $T(6) = \infty$.

1. $T(2) = MIN[T(2), P(1) + b_{12}] = 280$

   $T(3) = MIN[T(3), P(1) + b_{13}] = 410$

   $T(4) = MIN[T(4), P(1) + b_{14}] = 600$

   $T(5) = MIN[T(5), P(1) + b_{15}] = 870$

   $T(6) = MIN[T(6), P(1) + b_{16}] = 1260$

   PRIOR (2) = 1
   PRIOR (3) = 1
   PRIOR (4) = 1   Since nodes 2-6 had their temporary labels
   PRIOR (5) = 1   changed using node 1
   PRIOR (6) = 1

   MIN[280, 410, 600, 870, 1260] = 280, so node 2 gets a permanent label: $P(2) = 280$.

2) $T(3) = MIN[T(3), P(2) + b_{23}] = MIN[410, 280 + 290] = 410$

   $T(4) = MIN[T(4), P(2) + b_{24}] = MIN[600, 280 + 420] = 600$

   $T(5) = MIN[T(5), P(2) + b_{25}] = MIN[870, 280 + 610] = 870$

   $T(6) = MIN[T(6), P(2) + b_{26}] = MIN[1260, 280 + 880] = 1160$

   Since only node 6 had its temporary label changed, we set PRIOR(6) = 2.

   MIN[410, 600, 870, 1160] = 410, so node 3 gets a permanent label: $P(3) = 410$.

3. $T(4) = MIN[T(4), P(3) + b_{34}] = MIN[600, 410 + 310] = 600$

   $T(5) = MIN[T(5), P(3) + b_{35}] = MIN[870, 410 + 440] = 850$

   $T(6) = MIN[T(6), P(3) + b_{36}] = MIN[1160, 410 + 630] = 1040$

   Since nodes 5 and 6 had their temporary labels changed, we set

       PRIOR(5) = 3
       PRIOR(6) = 3

   MIN[600, 850, 1040] = 600, so $P(4) = 600$.

4. $T(5) = MIN[T(5), P(4) + b_{45}] = MIN[850, 600 + 320] = 850$
$T(6) = MIN[T(6), P(4) + b_{46}] = MIN[1040, 600 + 450] = 1040$

No nodes had their temporary labels changed, so PRIOR is not changed. $MIN[850, 1040] = 850$, so $P(5) = 850$.

5. $T(6) = MIN[T(6), P(5) + b_{56}] = MIN[1040, 850 + 340] = 1040$

PRIOR (6) is not changed; $P(6) = 1040$.

Since node 6 is permanently labelled, we are done. PRIOR(6) = 3 and PRIOR(3) = 1, and so the shortest path is $1 \rightarrow 3 \rightarrow 6$ with a cost of $1,040,000.

These new aircraft are purchased at the beginning of years 1 and 3.

Let x_{ij} = number of units of milk shipped from farm i to dealer j.

Minimize $9x_{11} + 4x_{12} + 5x_{13} + 11x_{14} + 3x_{15} + 14x_{16} + 12x_{17} + 2x_{18}$

$+ 13x_{19} + 1x_{1,10} + 11x_{21} + 15x_{22} + 1x_{23} + 7x_{24} + 12x_{25} + 8x_{26}$

$+ 9x_{27} + 13x_{28} + 8x_{29} + 7x_{2,10} + 5x_{31} + 4x_{32} + 8x_{33} + 14x_{34}$

$+ 11x_{35} + 10x_{36} + 2x_{37} + 13x_{38} + 15x_{39} + 6x_{3,10} + 9x_{41} + 10x_{42}$

$+ 5x_{43} + 10x_{44} + 3x_{45} + 7x_{46} + 12x_{47} + 14x_{48} + 6x_{49} + 3x_{4,10}$

Supply Constraints

$$x_{11} + x_{12} + x_{13} + x_{14} + x_{15} + x_{16} + x_{17} + x_{18} + x_{19} + x_{1,10} \leq 325$$
$$x_{21} + x_{22} + x_{23} + x_{24} + x_{25} + x_{26} + x_{27} + x_{28} + x_{29} + x_{2,10} \leq 175$$
$$x_{31} + x_{32} + x_{33} + x_{34} + x_{35} + x_{36} + x_{37} + x_{38} + x_{39} + x_{3,10} \leq 225$$
$$x_{41} + x_{42} + x_{43} + x_{44} + x_{45} + x_{46} + x_{47} + x_{48} + x_{49} + x_{4,10} \leq 160$$

Demand Constraints

$$x_{11} + x_{21} + x_{31} + x_{41} = 40$$
$$x_{12} + x_{22} + x_{32} + x_{42} = 70$$
$$x_{13} + x_{23} + x_{33} + x_{43} = 30$$
$$x_{14} + x_{24} + x_{34} + x_{44} = 110$$
$$x_{15} + x_{25} + x_{35} + x_{45} = 60$$
$$x_{16} + x_{26} + x_{36} + x_{46} = 80$$
$$x_{17} + x_{27} + x_{37} + x_{47} = 50$$
$$x_{18} + x_{28} + x_{38} + x_{48} = 100$$
$$x_{19} + x_{29} + x_{39} + x_{49} = 20$$
$$x_{1,10} + x_{2,10} + x_{3,10} + x_{4,10} = 90$$

$x_{ij} \geq 0$ for i=1, 2, 3, 4 and j=1, 2,..., 10

11.
This can be viewed as a transportation problem with 4 supply points, 5 demand points and the following shipping costs (d_{ij}) for i=1, 2, 3, 4 and j=1, 2, 3, 4, 5

Destinations

		1 Dallas	2 Los Angeles	3 Miami	4 New York	5 St. Louis	Supplies
1	Chicago	936	2075	1349	806	285	45
2	Denver	785	1102	2010	1756	851	20
3	Houston	245	1529	1199	1612	837	90
4	Memphis	472	1801	972	1079	277	55
	Demands	50	25	35	40	60	

Sources (3 Houston, 4 Memphis rows)

Let x_{ij} = number of cars shipped from i to j

OBJECTIVE FUNCTION

Minimize $\sum_{i=1}^{4} \sum_{j=1}^{5} d_{ij} x_{ij}$ where the d_{ij} are given in the table above

DEMAND CONSTRAINTS

$\sum_{i=1}^{4} x_{ij} = d_j$ j=1, 2,..., 5

where
$$d_1 = 50$$
$$d_2 = 25$$
$$d_3 = 35$$
$$d_4 = 40$$
$$d_5 = 60$$

SUPPLY CONSTRAINTS

$\sum_{j=1}^{5} x_{ij} = s_i$ i=1, 2, 3, 4

where
$$s_1 = 45$$
$$s_2 = 20$$
$$s_3 = 90$$
$$s_4 = 55$$

and x_{ij} = 0, 1, 2,...   for i=1, 2, 3, 4 and j=1, 2, 3, 4, 5

-78-

#12 Let x_{Ai} = number of bicycles assembled at plant A for dealer i

   x_{Bi} = number of bicycles assembled at plant B for dealer i where
      i=1, 2, 3, 4

   The total costs can be obtained by adding on the assembly costs to the shipping costs. These are shown in the table below.

TOTAL COSTS

DEALER

Assembly Plant	1	2	3	4
A	55	48	51	63
B	57	72	70	62

   The transportation model can now be formulated as:

Minimize: $55x_{A1} + 48x_{A2} + 51x_{A3} + 63x_{A4}$

         $+ 57x_{B1} + 72x_{B2} + 70x_{B3} + 62x_{B4}$

Subject to:

   $x_{A1} + x_{A2} + x_{A3} + x_{A4} \leq 1100$ Supply constraints
   $x_{B1} + x_{B2} + x_{B3} + x_{B4} \leq 1000$

   $x_{A1} + x_{B1} = 600$
   $x_{A2} + x_{B2} = 200$ Demand Constraints
   $x_{A3} + x_{B3} = 500$
   $x_{A4} + x_{B4} = 700$

   $x_{Ai}, x_{Bi} = 0, 1, 2, 3,\ldots$ for i=1, 2, 3, 4

Let x_{Ai} = number of bicycles assembled at plant A for dealer i

x_{Bi} = number of bicycles assembled at plant B for dealer i
where i=1, 2, 3, 4

Since the total demand exceeds the total supply, a fictitious assembly plant, C, needs to be added.

Let x_{Ci} = number of bicycles assembled at plant C for dealer i

The objective function coefficients of x_{Ai} and x_{Bi} will be the profit realized by shipping one bicycle from plant A or B to dealer i. This can be expressed as the selling price at i minus the assembly cost at A or B minus the shipping cost from A or B to i. Also, the profit realized for shipments from fictitious source to any dealer is 0.

The transportation problem can then be formulated as:

Maximize: $(100-45-10)x_{A1} + (95-45-3)x_{A2} + (105-45-6)x_{A3}$

$+ (100-45-18)x_{A4} + (100-55-2)x_{B1} + (95-55-17)x_{B2}$

$+ (105-55-15)x_{B3} + (100-55-7)x_{B4}$

or

Maximize: $45x_{A1} + 47x_{A2} + 54x_{A3} + 37x_{A4} + 43x_{B1} + 23x_{B2}$

$+ 35x_{B3} + 38x_{B4}$

Subject to:

$x_{A1} + x_{A2} + x_{A3} + x_{A4} = 1100$

$x_{B1} + x_{B2} + x_{B3} + x_{B4} = 1000$ Supply Constraints

$x_{C1} + x_{C2} + x_{C3} + x_{C4} = 100$

$x_{A1} + x_{B1} + x_{C1} = 660$

$x_{A2} + x_{B2} + x_{C2} = 220$ Demand Constraints

$x_{A3} + x_{B3} + x_{C3} = 550$

$x_{A4} + x_{B4} + x_{C4} = 770$

$x_{Ai}, x_{Bi}, x_{Ci} = 0, 1, 2,\ldots$ for i=1, 2, 3, 4

Let x_{ij} = number of units shipped from supply point i to demand
point j that are produced on regular time.

y_{ij} = number of units shipped from supply point i to demand
point j that are produced on overtime

Adding production costs to shipping costs, we have

Minimize: $54x_{A1} + 52x_{A2} + 53x_{A3} + 51x_{A4} + 54x_{A5}$

$+ 66x_{B1} + 61x_{B2} + 63x_{B3} + 62x_{B4} + 62x_{B5}$

$+ 79y_{A1} + 77y_{A2} + 78y_{A3} + 76y_{A4} + 79y_{A5}$

$+ 96y_{B1} + 91y_{B2} + 93y_{B3} + 92y_{B4} + 92y_{B5}$

Subject to:

$$x_{A1} + x_{B1} + y_{A1} + y_{B1} = 300$$
$$x_{A2} + x_{B2} + y_{A2} + y_{B2} = 500$$
$$x_{A3} + x_{B3} + y_{A3} + y_{B3} = 400 \qquad \text{Demand}$$
$$x_{A4} + x_{B4} + y_{A4} + y_{B4} = 300 \qquad \text{Constraints}$$
$$x_{A5} + x_{B5} + y_{A5} + y_{B5} = 300$$

$$x_{A1} + x_{A2} + x_{A3} + x_{A4} + x_{A5} \leq 1000 \qquad \text{Regular time}$$
$$x_{B1} + x_{B2} + x_{B3} + x_{B4} + x_{B5} \leq 800 \qquad \text{capacity constraints}$$

$$y_{A1} + y_{A2} + y_{A3} + y_{A4} + y_{A5} \leq 100 \qquad \text{Overtime capacity}$$
$$y_{B1} + y_{B2} + y_{B3} + y_{B4} + y_{B5} \leq 80 \qquad \text{constraints}$$

$x_{ij} = 0, 1, 2, \ldots$ for i=A, B and j=1, 2, 3, 4, 5

$y_{ij} = 0, 1, 2, \ldots$ for i=A, B and j=1, 2, 3, 4, 5

It should be observed that since overtime costs are higher than
regular time costs, the optimal solution will never utilize overtime
production unless regular time production at the same plant is fully
utilized.

ORDER

Months before	1	2	3	4	5
Delivery	0	1	2	3	4

Let x_{ij} = 1, if batch i is used for order j
0, if batch i is not used for order j

For example, if batch 1 is used for order 2, it will be two months old, and the profit will be $p_2(2)=50$. Similarly, if batch 2 is used for order 1, it will be three months old, and the profit will be $p_1(3)=17$.

The problem can be formulated as:

Minimize: $35x_{11} + 50x_{12} + 30x_{13} + 7x_{14} + 17x_{15}$

$+ 17x_{21} + 47x_{22} + 30x_{23} + 7x_{24} + 15x_{25}$

$+ 20x_{31} + 49x_{32} + 30x_{33} + 7x_{34} + 15x_{35}$

$+ 35x_{41} + 50x_{42} + 30x_{43} + 7x_{44} + 17x_{45}$

$+ 16x_{51} + 45x_{52} + 30x_{53} + 6x_{54} + 14x_{55}$

Subject to:

$$x_{11} + x_{12} + x_{13} + x_{14} + x_{15} = 1$$
$$x_{21} + x_{22} + x_{23} + x_{24} + x_{25} = 1$$
$$x_{31} + x_{32} + x_{33} + x_{34} + x_{35} = 1 \quad \text{Supply}$$
$$x_{41} + x_{42} + x_{43} + x_{44} + x_{45} = 1 \quad \text{constraints}$$
$$x_{51} + x_{52} + x_{53} + x_{54} + x_{55} = 1$$

$$x_{11} + x_{21} + x_{31} + x_{41} + x_{51} = 1$$
$$x_{12} + x_{22} + x_{32} + x_{42} + x_{52} = 1$$
$$x_{13} + x_{23} + x_{33} + x_{43} + x_{53} = 1 \quad \text{Demand}$$
$$x_{14} + x_{24} + x_{34} + x_{44} + x_{54} = 1 \quad \text{constraints}$$
$$x_{15} + x_{25} + x_{35} + x_{45} + x_{55} = 1$$

$x_{ij} = 0, 1$ for i=1, 2, 3, 4, 5 and j=1, 2, 3, 4, 5

#16   Note to instructor: Because of the difficulty in grading this problem if students do not all use the same format, it is suggested that you give them this format as a guideline.

     The shortest paths are obtained by inspection as shown below.

ORIGIN	DESTINATION	PATH	FLOW
1	2	$1 \to 2$	8
1	3	$1 \to 2 \to 3$	6
1	4	$1 \to 4$	7
1	5	$1 \to 5$	3
1	6	$1 \to 5 \to 6$	1
1	7	$1 \to 4 \to 7$	4
1	8	$1 \to 5 \to 8$	2
1	9	$1 \to 5 \to 6 \to 9$	6
2	3	$2 \to 3$	1
2	4	$2 \to 1 \to 4$	2
2	5	$2 \to 6 \to 5$	7
2	6	$2 \to 6$	6
2	7	$2 \to 1 \to 4 \to 7$	3
2	8	$2 \to 6 \to 9 \to 8$	1
2	9	$2 \to 6 \to 9$	2
3	4	$3 \to 6 \to 5 \to 4$	8
3	5	$3 \to 6 \to 5$	10
3	6	$3 \to 6$	12
3	7	$3 \to 6 \to 5 \to 4 \to 7$	4
3	8	$3 \to 6 \to 9 \to 8$	9
3	9	$3 \to 6 \to 9$	6
4	5	$4 \to 5$	1
4	6	$4 \to 5 \to 6$	1
4	7	$4 \to 7$	3
4	8	$4 \to 5 \to 8$	2
4	9	$4 \to 5 \to 6 \to 9$	1
5	6	$5 \to 6$	5
5	7	$5 \to 4 \to 7$	4
5	8	$5 \to 8$	2
5	9	$5 \to 6 \to 9$	3
6	7	$6 \to 5 \to 4 \to 7$	9
6	8	$6 \to 9 \to 8$	8
6	9	$6 \to 9$	3
7	8	$7 \to 8$	6
7	9	$7 \to 4 \to 5 \to 6 \to 9$	1
8	9	$8 \to 9$	2

     It should be noted that the shortest path between nodes i and j where $j < i$ is the reverse of the path from i to j. The above table, then, gives the shortest path between each pair of nodes.

16(cont)   Assigning flows to the shortest paths results in arc flows of:

ARCS   FLOW

(1,2) and (2,1)   8 + 6 + 2 + 3 = 19
(1,4) and (4,1)   7 + 4 + 2 + 3 = 16
(1,5) and (5,1)   3 + 1 + 2 + 6 = 12
(2,3) and (3,2)   6 + 1 = 7
(2,6) and (6,2)   7 + 6 + 1 + 2 = 16
(3,6) and (6,3)   8 + 10 + 12 + 4 + 9 + 6 = 49
(4,5) and (5,4)   8 + 4 + 1 + 1 + 2 + 1 + 4 + 9 + 1 = 31
(4,7) and (7,4)   4 + 3 + 4 + 3 + 4 + 9 + 1 = 28
(5,6) and (6,5)   1 + 6 + 7 + 8 + 10 + 4 + 1 + 5 + 3 + 9 + 1 = 56
(5,8) and (8,5)   2 + 2 + 2 = 6
(6,9) and (9,6)   6 + 1 + 2 + 9 + 6 + 1 + 3 + 8 + 3 + 1 = 40
(7,8) and (8,7)   6
(8,9) and (9,8)   1 + 9 + 8 + 2 = 20

   The above table gives the traffic flow along each arc for the
future period.

Using the notation described in the problem, we have:

Minimize:

$$0(x_{11} + y_{11}) + 20(x_{12} + y_{12}) + 15(x_{13} + y_{13}) + 12(x_{14} + y_{14})$$

$$+ 10(x_{15} + y_{15}) + 20(x_{21} + y_{21}) + 0(x_{22} + y_{22}) + 10(x_{23} + y_{23})$$

$$+ 7(x_{24} + y_{24}) + 25(x_{25} + y_{25}) + 15(x_{31} + y_{31}) + 10(x_{32} + y_{32})$$

$$+ 0(x_{33} + y_{33}) + 16(x_{34} + y_{34}) + 18(x_{35} + y_{35}) + 12(x_{41} + y_{41})$$

$$+ 7(x_{42} + y_{42}) + 16(x_{43} + y_{43}) + 0(x_{44} + y_{44}) + 13(x_{45} + y_{45})$$

$$+ 10(x_{51} + y_{51}) + 25(x_{52} + y_{52}) + 18(x_{53} + y_{53}) + 13(x_{54} + x_{54})$$

$$+ 0(x_{55} + y_{55})$$

Subject to:

$$\sum_{j=1}^{5} y_{1j} = 1{,}563$$

$$\sum_{j=1}^{5} y_{2j} = 1{,}250$$

$$\sum_{j=1}^{5} y_{3j} = 1{,}175 \qquad \text{Black students'}$$
$$\text{demand constraints}$$

$$\sum_{j=1}^{5} y_{4j} = 1{,}408$$

$$\sum_{j=1}^{5} y_{5j} = 2{,}502$$

$$\sum_{j=1}^{5} x_{1j} = 3{,}052$$

$$\sum_{j=1}^{5} x_{2j} = 2{,}507$$

$$\sum_{j=1}^{5} x_{3j} = 2{,}875 \qquad \text{White students'}$$
$$\text{demand constraints}$$

$$\sum_{j=1}^{5} x_{4j} = 1{,}076$$

$$\sum_{j=1}^{5} x_{5j} = 851$$

17 (cont) $\sum\limits_{i=1}^{5} (x_{i1} + y_{i1}) \leq 5{,}000$

$\sum\limits_{i=1}^{5} (x_{i2} + y_{i2}) \leq 6{,}500$

$\sum\limits_{i=1}^{5} (x_{i3} + y_{i3}) \leq 3{,}500$ School capacity
constraints

$\sum\limits_{i=1}^{5} (x_{i4} + y_{i4}) \leq 4{,}500$

$\sum\limits_{i=1}^{5} (x_{i5} + y_{i5}) \leq 4{,}000$

$$\dfrac{\sum\limits_{i=1}^{5} y_{ij}}{\sum\limits_{i=1}^{5} (x_{ij} + y_{ij})} \leq 0.53 \qquad \text{for } j=1, 2, 3, 4, 5$$

that is,

$$\sum\limits_{i=1}^{5} y_{ij} \leq 0.53 \, [\, \sum\limits_{i=1}^{5} (x_{ij} + y_{ij})] \qquad \text{for } j=1, 2, 3, 4, 5$$

and

$$\dfrac{\sum\limits_{i=1}^{5} y_{ij}}{\sum\limits_{i=1}^{5} (x_{ij} + y_{ij})} \geq 0.33 \qquad \text{for } j=1, 2, 3, 4, 5$$

that is,

$$\sum\limits_{i=1}^{5} y_{ij} \geq 0.33 \, [\, \sum\limits_{i=1}^{5} (x_{ij} + y_{ij})] \qquad \text{for } j=1, 2, 3, 4, 5$$

$x_{ij}, \; y_{ij} = 0, 1, 2, \ldots \qquad \text{for } i,j=1, 2, 3, 4, 5$

Let x_{ij} = number of messages per minute actually flowing from
node i to node j
y_{ij} = increase in capacity of arc (i,j)

Minimize: $5y_{12} + 6y_{13} + 4y_{32} + 7y_{24} + 5y_{34} + 6y_{45} + 10y_{35}$

$+ 0x_{12} + 0x_{13} + 0x_{32} + 0x_{24} + 0x_{34} + 0x_{45} + 0x_{35}$

Subject to:

$$x_{12} + x_{13} = 10$$
$$x_{12} + x_{32} = x_{24}$$
$$x_{13} = x_{32} + x_{34} + x_{35}$$
$$x_{24} + x_{34} = x_{45}$$
$$x_{35} + x_{45} = 10$$

Conservation of
flow constraints

$$x_{12} \le 3 + y_{12}$$
$$x_{13} \le 4 + y_{13}$$
$$x_{24} \le 4 + y_{24}$$
$$x_{32} \le 1 + y_{32}$$
$$x_{34} \le 3 + y_{34}$$
$$x_{35} \le 3 + y_{35}$$
$$x_{45} \le 5 + y_{45}$$

Capacity constraints

x_{ij}, y_{ij} = 0, 1, 2, 3, 4,...   for i=1, 2, 3, 4 and j=2, 3, 4, 5

#19   Let x_{ij} = amount of garbage shipped from location i to dump j

Minimize: $$\sum_{i=1}^{n} \sum_{j=1}^{3} c_{ij}\, x_{ij}$$

Subject to $$\sum_{i=1}^{n} x_{ij} \leq C_j \qquad \text{for } j=1, 2,\ldots, N$$

$$\sum_{j=1}^{3} x_{ij} = P_i \qquad \text{for } i=1, 2,\ldots, n$$

$$x_{ij} \geq 0 \qquad \text{for all } i,j.$$

Let x_{ij} = number of trips per day (in units of 100) made from node i to node j.

OBJECTIVE FUNCTION

Minimize: $(4.5x_{12} + 4x_{14} + 2x_{15} + 4.5x_{21} + 3x_{23} + 2x_{26} + 3x_{32} + 2x_{36}$

$+ 4x_{41} + 5x_{45} + 1.5x_{47} + 2x_{51} + 5x_{54} + 4x_{56} + 3x_{58} + 2x_{62}$

$+ 2x_{63} + 4x_{65} + 1x_{69} + 1.5x_{74} + 7x_{78} + 3x_{85} + 7x_{87} + 5x_{89} + 1x_{96} + 5x_{98})$

$+ (5x_{16} + 7x_{19} + 9x_{27} + 4x_{48} + 5x_{61} + 9x_{72} + 4x_{84} + 7x_{91})$

Here the last 8 terms represent congestion on proposed arcs, and the other terms represent congestion on existing arcs.

BUDGET CONSTRAINT

$$400,000y_1 + 500,000y_2 + 600,000y_3 + 300,000y_4 \leq 1,000,000$$

where $y_i = 0$ implies no flow on the arc
and $y_i = 1$ implies any amount of flow on the arc

CONSERVATION OF FLOW CONSTRAINTS

There will be 8 equations for each node. Shown below are the remaining conservation of flow equations for node 5.

$$3 + \quad + x_{45}^1 + x_{65}^1 + x_{85}^1 = x_{51}^1 + x_{54}^1 + x_{56}^1 + x_{58}^1$$

$$7 + x_{15}^2 + x_{45}^2 + x_{65}^2 + x_{85}^2 = x_{51}^2 + x_{54}^2 + x_{56}^2 + x_{58}^2$$

$$10 + x_{15}^3 + x_{45}^3 + x_{65}^3 + x_{85}^3 = x_{51}^3 + x_{54}^3 + x_{56}^3 + x_{58}^3$$

$$1 + x_{15}^4 + \quad + x_{65}^4 + x_{85}^4 = x_{51}^4 + x_{54}^4 + x_{56}^4 + x_{58}^4$$

$$5 + x_{15}^6 + x_{45}^6 + x_{65}^6 + x_{85}^6 = x_{51}^6 + x_{54}^6 + x_{56}^6 + x_{58}^6$$

$$4 + x_{15}^7 + x_{45}^7 + x_{65}^7 + x_{85}^7 = x_{51}^7 + x_{54}^7 + x_{56}^7 + x_{58}^7$$

$$3 + x_{15}^9 + x_{45}^9 + x_{65}^9 + x_{85}^9 = x_{51}^9 + x_{54}^9 + x_{56}^9 + x_{58}^9$$

Let M be the maximum number of trips per day (in units of 100) that can be made on any of the proposed highway. For example, M = 318 (the sum of all the trip table elements) will suffice. Then,

$$x_{16} + x_{61} \leq My_1$$

$$x_{19} + x_{91} \leq My_2$$

$$x_{27} + x_{72} \leq My_3$$

$$x_{48} + x_{84} \leq My_4$$

$$x_{ij} \geq 0 \qquad \text{for all arcs } (i,j).$$

Let x_{ij} = flow on arc (i,j)

     $c_{ij} \sqrt{x_{ij}}$ = shipping cost on arc (i,j)

OBJECTIVE FUNCTION

Minimize: $c_{12} \sqrt{x_{12}} + c_{13} \sqrt{x_{13}} + c_{14} \sqrt{x_{14}} + c_{24} \sqrt{x_{24}}$

     $+ c_{27} \sqrt{x_{27}} + c_{35} \sqrt{x_{35}} + c_{46} \sqrt{x_{46}} + c_{56} \sqrt{x_{56}} + c_{58} \sqrt{x_{58}}$

     $+ c_{67} \sqrt{x_{67}} + c_{6,10} \sqrt{x_{6,10}} + c_{7,10} \sqrt{x_{7,10}} + c_{89} \sqrt{x_{89}} + c_{9,10} \sqrt{x_{9,10}}$

CONSTRAINTS

Node (1):	$x_{12} + x_{13} + x_{14} = 100$
Node (2):	$x_{12} = x_{24} + x_{27}$
Node (3):	$x_{13} = x_{35}$
Node (4):	$x_{14} + x_{24} = x_{46}$
Node (5):	$x_{35} = x_{56} + x_{58}$
Node (6):	$x_{46} + x_{56} = x_{67} + x_{6,10}$
Node (7):	$x_{27} + x_{67} = x_{7,10}$
Node (8):	$x_{58} = x_{89}$
Node (9):	$x_{89} = x_{9,10}$
Node (10):	$x_{6,10} + x_{7,10} + x_{9,10} = 100$

NON-NEGATIVITY CONSTRAINTS

     $x_{ij} \geq 0$ all arcs (i,j)

22. Let x_{ij} = number of kilowatts of electricity leaving node i on arc (i,j)

Maximize $\qquad$ f
$\quad$ x,f

subject to $\qquad\qquad\qquad .98x_{12} = x_{25} + x_{24}$ $\qquad\qquad$ (node 2)

$\qquad\qquad\qquad\qquad\qquad .98x_{13} = x_{34} + x_{35}$ $\qquad\qquad$ (node 3)

$\qquad\qquad\qquad\qquad\qquad .96x_{24} + 0.98x_{34} = x_{46} + x_{47}$ $\qquad$ (node 4)

$\qquad\qquad\qquad\qquad\qquad .98x_{25} + 0.94x_{35} = x_{56}$ $\qquad\qquad$ (node 5)

$\qquad\qquad\qquad\qquad\qquad .98x_{46} + 0.98x_{56} = x_{68}$ $\qquad\qquad$ (node 6)

$\qquad\qquad\qquad\qquad\qquad .96x_{47} = x_{78}$ $\qquad\qquad\qquad$ (node 7)

$\qquad\qquad\qquad\qquad\qquad .96x_{68} + .97x_{78} = f$ $\qquad\qquad$ (node 8)

$\qquad\qquad\qquad\qquad\qquad x_{12} \leq 200$

$\qquad\qquad\qquad\qquad\qquad x_{13} \leq 100$

$\qquad\qquad\qquad\qquad\qquad x_{24} \leq 200$

$\qquad\qquad\qquad\qquad\qquad x_{25} \leq 100$

$\qquad\qquad\qquad\qquad\qquad x_{34} \leq 50$ $\qquad\qquad\qquad$ Capacity

$\qquad\qquad\qquad\qquad\qquad x_{35} \leq 150$ $\qquad\qquad\qquad$ Constraints

$\qquad\qquad\qquad\qquad\qquad x_{46} \leq 125$

$\qquad\qquad\qquad\qquad\qquad x_{47} \leq 50$

$\qquad\qquad\qquad\qquad\qquad x_{56} \leq 150$

$\qquad\qquad\qquad\qquad\qquad x_{68} \leq 100$

$\qquad\qquad\qquad\qquad\qquad x_{78} \leq 200$

$f, x_{ij} \geq 0$ $\quad$ for all arcs (i,j)

23. Let c_{ij} = cost of shipping 1 ton of pulp from i to j

   b_{jk} = cost of shipping 1 unit of any product from j to k

Also x_{ij}^p is measured in tons while z_{jk}^p is in units of product p.

OBJECTIVE FUNCTION

Minimize: $$\sum_{i=1}^{3} \sum_{j=1}^{2} c_{ij} \sum_{p=1}^{4} x_{ij}^p + \sum_{j=1}^{2} \sum_{k=1}^{3} b_{jk} \sum_{p=1}^{4} z_{jk}^p$$

CONSTRAINTS

$$\sum_{j=1}^{2} x_{ij}^p \leq S_i^p \qquad \text{i=1, 2, 3; p=1, 2, 3, 4}$$

   Where S_i^p denotes the number of tons available at forest i to be converted to product p.

$$\sum_{i=1}^{3} A_p x_{ij}^p = \sum_{k=1}^{3} z_{jk}^p \qquad \text{j=1, 2; p=1, 2, 3, 4}$$

$$\sum_{j=1}^{2} z_{jk}^p = D_k^p \qquad \text{k=1, 2, 3; p=1, 2, 3, 4}$$

$$\sum_{p=1}^{4} z_{jk}^p \leq U_{jk} \qquad \text{j=1, 2; k=1, 2, 3}$$

$$x_{ij}^p, z_{jk}^p \geq 0 \qquad \begin{array}{l} \text{i=1, 2, 3; j=1, 2} \\ \text{k=1, 2, 3; p=1, 2, 3, 4} \end{array}$$

24. Let ℓ_{jk} = length of arc (i,j) in miles

   y_{jk} = number of watts transmitted from station (or city) j to city k

   x_{ij} = number of tons of coal sent from mine i to station j

   S_i = supply of coal available at mine i in tons

   D_k = demand, in watts, of city p

OBJECTIVE FUNCTION

Minimize $b_{14}x_{14} + b_{15}x_{15} + b_{24}x_{24} + b_{25}x_{25} + b_{34}x_{34} + b_{35}x_{35}$

$+ c_{46}y_{46} + c_{47}y_{47} + c_{48}y_{48} + c_{56}y_{56} + c_{59}y_{59} + c_{5,10}y_{5,10} + c_{5,11}y_{5,11}$

$+ c_{69}y_{69} + c_{78}y_{78} + c_{87}y_{87} + c_{96}y_{96} + c_{10,11}y_{10,11} + c_{10,12}y_{10,12}$

$+ c_{11,10}y_{11,10} + c_{11,12}y_{11,12} + c_{12,10}y_{12,10} + c_{12,11}y_{12,11}$

CONSTRAINTS FOR THE MINES

$x_{14} + x_{15} \leq S_1$

$x_{24} + x_{25} \leq S_2$

$x_{34} + x_{35} \leq S_3$

CONSTRAINTS FOR THE STATIONS

$B_1 x_{14} + B_2 x_{24} + B_3 x_{34} = y_{46} + y_{47} + y_{48}$

$B_1 x_{15} + B_2 x_{25} + B_3 x_{35} = y_{56} + y_{59} + y_{5,10} + y_{5,11}$

CONSTRAINTS FOR THE CITIES

$y_{46}(0 \cdot 9)^{\ell_{46}} + y_{56}(0 \cdot 9)^{\ell_{56}} + y_{96}(0 \cdot 9)^{\ell_{96}} = D_6 + y_{69}$

$y_{47}(0 \cdot 9)^{\ell_{47}} + y_{87}(0 \cdot 9)^{\ell_{87}} = D_7 + y_{78}$

$y_{48}(0 \cdot 9)^{\ell_{48}} + y_{78}(0 \cdot 9)^{\ell_{78}} = D_8 + y_{87}$

$y_{59}(0 \cdot 9)^{\ell_{59}} + y_{69}(0 \cdot 9)^{\ell_{69}} = D_9 + y_{96}$

$y_{5,10}(0 \cdot 9)^{\ell_{5,10}} + y_{11,10}(0 \cdot 9)^{\ell_{11,10}} + y_{12,10}(0 \cdot 9)^{\ell_{12,10}}$

$= D_{10} + y_{10,11} + y_{10,12}$

CONSTRAINTS FOR THE CITIES (cont)

$$y_{5,11}(0.9)^{\ell_{5,11}} + y_{10,11}(0.9)^{\ell_{10,11}} + y_{12,11}(0.9)^{\ell_{12,11}}$$

$$= D_{11} + y_{11,10} + y_{11,12}$$

$$y_{10,12}(0.9)^{\ell_{10,12}} + y_{11,12}(0.9)^{\ell_{11,12}} = D_{12} + y_{12,10} + y_{12,11}$$

NON-NEGATIVITY CONSTRAINTS

$$x_{ij}, \; y_{jk} \geq 0 \qquad\qquad \text{for all arcs } (i,j) \text{ and } (j,k)$$

25. Let x_{ij} = amount shipped from supply point i to demand point j

$$y_i = \begin{cases} 1 \text{ if plant i is constructed, } i=4, 5, 6 \\ 0 \text{ otherwise} \end{cases}$$

OBJECTIVE FUNCTION

$$\text{Minimize} \quad \sum_{i=1}^{6} \sum_{j=1}^{9} c_{ij}x_{ij} + 1,000,000y_4 + 850,000y_5 + 1,250,000y_6$$

DEMAND CONSTRAINTS

$$\sum_{i=1}^{6} x_{ij} = D_j \qquad\qquad j=1, 2,\ldots,9$$

SUPPLY CONSTRAINTS

$$\sum_{j=1}^{9} x_{ij} \leq S_i \qquad\qquad i=1, 2, 3$$

$$\sum_{j=1}^{9} x_{ij} \leq y_i S_i \qquad\qquad i=4, 5, 6$$

$$x_{ij} \geq 0 \qquad\qquad i=1, 2,\ldots,6 \quad \text{and} \quad j=1, 2,\ldots,9$$

$$y_i = 0 \text{ or } 1 \qquad\qquad i=4, 5, 6$$

26(a)

Let x_{ij}^{pq} = number of units of product q shipped from refinery i to satisfy customer j's demand for product p.

MAXIMIZE:
$$\sum_{i=1}^{m} \sum_{j=1}^{n} \sum_{p=1}^{200} \sum_{q=1}^{200} c_{ij}^{pq} \, x_{ij}^{pq}$$

such that

$$\sum_{p=1}^{200} \sum_{j=1}^{n} x_{ij}^{pq} \leq S_{iq} \qquad \begin{array}{l} i=1, 2,\ldots,m \\ q=1, 2,\ldots,200 \end{array}$$

$$\sum_{i=1}^{m} \sum_{q=1}^{200} x_{ij}^{pq} = D_{jp} \qquad \begin{array}{l} j=1, 2,\ldots,n \\ p=1, 2,\ldots,200 \end{array}$$

$$x_{ij}^{pq} \geq 0 \qquad \begin{array}{l} \text{for } i=1, 2,\ldots,m; \quad j=1, 2,\ldots,n \\ p=1, 2,\ldots,200; \quad q=1, 2,\ldots,200 \end{array}$$

26(b)

The total demand for all products by customer j is $\sum_{p=1}^{200} D_{jp}$.
The total amount received by customer j which is acceptable is

$$\sum_{i=1}^{m} \sum_{p=1}^{200} \sum_{q \in A_{jp}} x_{ij}^{pq} \quad \text{where } A_{jp} \equiv \text{products acceptable to customer j as a substitute for product p.}$$

Therefore the added constraints are

$$\frac{\sum_{i=1}^{m} \sum_{p=1}^{200} \sum_{q \in A_{1p}} x_{i1}^{pq}}{\sum_{p=1}^{200} D_{1p}} = \frac{\sum_{i=1}^{m} \sum_{p=1}^{200} \sum_{q \in A_{2p}} x_{i2}^{pq}}{\sum_{p=1}^{200} D_{2p}} = \ldots = \frac{\sum_{i=1}^{m} \sum_{p=1}^{200} \sum_{q \in A_{np}} x_{in}^{pq}}{\sum_{p=1}^{200} D_{np}}$$

for q=1, 2,...,200

Observe that there are 200 n added constraints.

27.

MAXIMIZE: $(1.08)^3 x_{11} + (1.07)(1.075)^2 x_{12} + (1.07)^2(1.09)x_{13}$

$+ (1.07)(1.081)^2 x_{14} + (1.076)^3 x_{15} + (1.07)(1.08)^2 x_{16}$

$+ (1.06)^3 x_{17} + (1.07)^2(1.07)x_{18} + (1.075)^2 x_{22}$

$+ (1.07)(1.09)x_{23} + (1.081)^2 x_{24} + (1.08)^2 x_{26}$

$+ (1.07)(1.07)x_{28} + (1.09)x_{33} + (1.07)x_{38}$

subject to:

$x_{11} + x_{12} + x_{13} + x_{14} + x_{15} + x_{16} + x_{17} + x_{18} \leq 100,000$

$x_{22} + x_{23} + x_{24} + x_{26} + x_{28} \leq 90,000$

$x_{33} + x_{38} \leq 125,000$

$x_{ij} \geq 0 \qquad$ all i,j

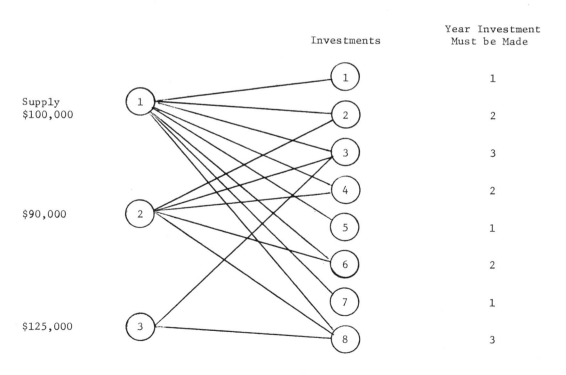

There is an arc from each supply point to each investment corresponding to the same year or to a later year than the supply point. Other arcs should be deleted from the model or may be included with large negative costs in the objective function.

28. Money can be "shipped" from year 1 to investments 1, 5, or 7, or to year 2. The costs for the first three arcs are $(1.08)^3$, $(1.076)^3$, and $(1.06)^3$, respectively.

   Money can be "shipped" from year 2 to investments 2, 4, or 6, or to year 3. Money can be "shipped" from year 3 to investments 3 or 8.

Maximize: $(1.08)^3 x_{11} + (1.076)^3 x_{15} + (1.06)^3 x_{17} + (1.075)^2 x_{22}$

   $+ (1.081)^2 x_{24} + (1.08)^2 x_{26} + (1.09) x_{33} + (1.07) x_{38}$

s.t. $x_{11} + x_{15} + x_{17} + y_{12} = 100{,}000$

   $x_{22} + x_{24} + x_{26} + y_{23} = 90{,}000 + (1.07) y_{12}$

   $x_{38} + x_{33} = 125{,}000 + (1.07) y_{23}$

   $x_{ij} \geq 0 \qquad \forall\ i,j$

29(a)

The amount of flow on each arc that maximizes the total flow of oil is shown below:

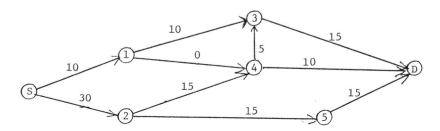

Hence the maximum amount of oil that can flow into D is 15 + 10 + 15 = 40.

It should be noted that alternative optima are possible.

29(b)

Since arcs (S,2), (2,4), (2,5), (1,3), (4,3), (4,D) have flow equal to capacity, these arcs should have their capacities increased.

30. The equivalent network is

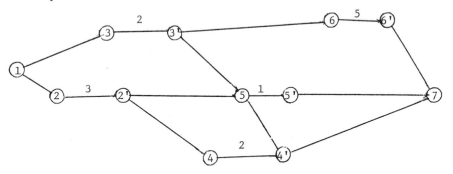

Non-zero arc lengths are shown in the figure.

The shortest path is 1→3→3'→5→5'→7.

31. Add a fictitious job 4 (applicant is rejected).

Let $x_{ij} = \begin{array}{l} 1, \text{ if applicant } i \text{ is assigned to job } j \\ 0, \text{ otherwise} \end{array}$

Maximize

$$0x_{11} + 6x_{12} + 7x_{13} + 0x_{14}$$
$$+ \quad 0x_{21} + 6x_{22} + 6x_{23} + 0x_{24}$$
$$+ \quad 5x_{31} + 8x_{32} + 0x_{33} + 0x_{34}$$
$$+ \quad 7x_{41} + 4x_{42} + 9x_{43} + 0x_{44}$$

st $\qquad \sum_{i=1}^{4} x_{ij} = 1 \qquad\qquad j=1, 2, 3, 4$

$\qquad \sum_{j=1}^{4} x_{ij} = 1 \qquad\qquad i=1, 2, 3, 4$

where $\qquad x_{ij} = 0,1$

Chapter 6

Problem 1

Source location: $(x,y) = (35.736, 24.490)$

Minimum cost = 340.39

Problem 2

Source location: $(x,y) = (22.706, 39.984)$

Minimum cost = 499.492

Problem 4

Source location: $(x,y) = (28.418, 55.315)$

Minimum cost = 3949.168

Problem 8

Source locations: $(x_1, y_1) = (18, 78)$

$(x_2, y_2) = (89, 65)$

Destinations 1,2,3,4 assigned to (x_1, y_1)

Destinations 5,6,7 assigned to (x_2, y_2)

Minimum sum of costs = 13,286.5

CHAPTER 7

1. The optimal sequence is $3, \to 7, \to 6, \to 4, \to 1, \to 2, \to 5$

   Note that the waiting times are

   $T_1 = P_3 + P_7 + P_6 + P_4 + P_1 = 31$

   $T_2 = P_3 + P_7 + P_6 + P_4 + P_1 + P_2 = 42$

   $T_3 = P_3 = 2$

   $T_4 = P_3 + P_7 + P_6 + P_4 = 21$

   $T_5 = P_3 + P_7 + P_6 + P_4 + P_1 + P_2 + P_5 = 56$

   $T_6 = P_3 + P_7 + P_6 = 13$

   $T_7 = P_3 + P_7 = 7$

   $$\text{Average time} = \frac{31 + 42 + 2 + 21 + 56 + 13 + 7}{7} = \frac{172}{7} = 24.6 \text{ hours}$$

2. The sequence that minimizes the average flow time is $1, \to 3, \to 4, \to 2, \to 5$

   Waiting times are

   $T_1 = P_1 = 1.5$

   $T_2 = P_1 + P_3 + P_4 + P_2 = 9.7$

   $T_3 = P_1 + P_3 = 3.5$

   $T_4 = P_1 + P_3 + P_4 = 6.0$

   $T_5 = P_1 + P_3 + P_4 + P_2 + P_5 = 13.95$

3. The sequence that minimizes the total time span is $3, \to 1, \to 6, \to 2, \to 5, \to 4$

   The corresponding Gantt chart is:

   | Phase 1 | 3 | 1 | 6 | 2 | 5 | 4 |
   | Phase 2 | | 3 | 1 | 6 | 2 | 5 | 4 |

-102-

4. The sequence which minimizes the total time span is $2, \to 3, \to 7, \to 5, \to 1, \to 6, \to 4$

The corresponding Gantt Chart is

Drill Press	2	3	7	5	1	6	4	

Grinder		2	3	7	5	1	6	4

Idle time for drill press = 0

Idle time for grinder is that shown by the shaded areas in the Gantt chart. (Initial idle time for the Grinder could also be counted). Its value is

= (5.1 - 3.4) + (9.1 - 8.2) + (9.9 - 7.4) + (6.7 - 6.3)
= 1.7 + 0.9 + 2.5 + 0.4
= 5.5 hours.

5.

Job	Lathe	Milling Machine	Progressing Sequence for Jobs	
1	12	8	First	3
2	0	18	Second	2
3	0	12	Third	6
4	5	0	Fourth	1
5	11	0	Fifth	5
6	10	9	Sixth	4

Therefore, a schedule that minimizes the total time span is $3, \to 2, \to 6, \to 1, \to 5, \to 4$

The corresponding Gantt chart is below. Note that there is no idle time.

Lathe	6	1	5	4	

Milling Machine	3	2	6	1

There is more than one optimal solution to the problem because of ties existing when choosing the initial job to be scheduled.

6.

Job	Injection Nozzles	Turbines	Progressing Sequence	
A	4	2	First	C
B	3	1	Second	A
C	5	3.5	Third	B

The optimum sequence which minimizes total time span is $C, \to A, \to A, \to B, \to B$

It should be observed that the number of engines of each type will not affect the solution to the problem.

-103-

7. Let x_{ij} = time at which operation i starts on job j (decision variable)
    t_{ij} = processing time of operation i on job j (constant)

    Minimize z

    s. t. $x_{2j} \geq x_{1j} + t_{1j}$ j=1, 2, 3, 4, 5

    or $\begin{cases} x_{ij} + t_{ij} \leq x_{iJ} \\ \\ x_{iJ} + t_{iJ} \leq x_{ij} \end{cases}$ i=1, 2, 3, 4; j, J=1, 2, 3, 4, 5; j≠J

    $z \geq x_{ij} + t_{ij}$ i=1, 2, 3, 4; j=1, 2, 3, 4, 5

    $x_{ij} \geq 0$ i=1, 2, 3, 4; j=1, 2, 3, 4, 5

8. The only two possible sequences are job 1, job 2 and job 2, job 1. If
    job 1 is processed first, both jobs are completed in 22 hours:

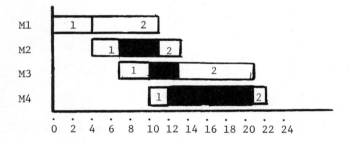

    If job 2 is processed first, both jobs are again completed in 22 hours:

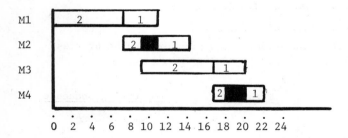

    Thus either sequence is optimal.

9. Let x_{ij} denote the time at which operation i starts on job j, j=1, 2, 3, 4, 5.
    Let t_{ij} denote the required processing time of operation i on job j
    (specified in the problem).

9. (cont.)

Here   Operation 1 is assembly,
                         Operation 2 is inspection,
                         Operation 3 is packing, and
                         Operation 4 is shipping.

Minimize z

subject to

$$z \geq x_{4j} + t_{4j} \qquad\qquad j=1, 2, 3, 4, 5$$

$$x_{ij} \geq x_{i-1,j} + t_{i-1,j} \qquad j=1, 2,\ldots,5 \text{ and } i=2, 3, 4$$

or
$$\begin{cases} x_{ij} + t_{ij} \leq x_{iJ} \\[2ex] x_{iJ} + t_{iJ} \leq x_{ij} \end{cases} \qquad \begin{aligned} &i=1, 2, 3, 4; \\ &j=1, 2, 3, 4, 5; \ j \neq J \end{aligned}$$

$$x_{ij} \geq 0 \qquad\qquad i=1, 2, 3, 4; \ j=1, 2, 3, 4, 5$$

10.

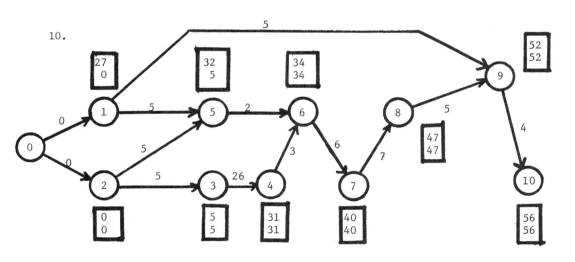

(a)   Critical path is $0 \to 2 \to 3 \to 4 \to 6 \to 7 \to 8 \to 9 \to 10$
       Critical path requires 56 days.

Let   ⬚   represent Earliest Start time
                represent Latest Start time

10 (b) <u>Slack Times</u>

Event	Slack
1	27
2	0
3	0
4	0
5	27
6	0
7	0
8	0
9	0

11.

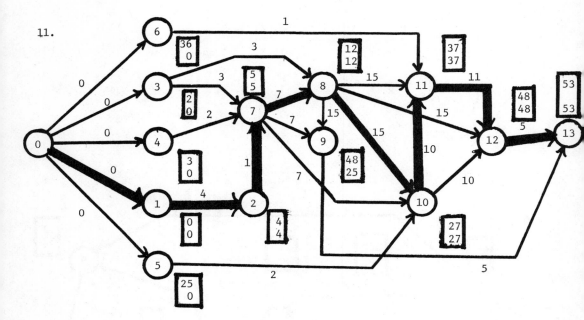

Note: □ : Latest Start time
         □ : Earliest Start time

Event	Slack
1	0
2	0
3	2
4	3
5	25
6	36
7	0
8	0
9	23
10	0
11	0
12	0

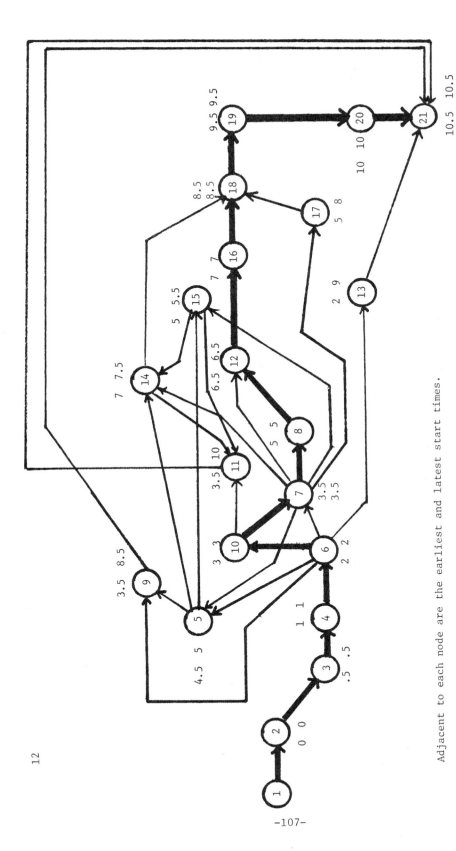

Adjacent to each node are the earliest and latest start times.

Arc lengths have been omitted; the length of the arc leaving each node i is the duration time of activity i.

12

12. (cont.)

Critical path is 1→2→3→4→6→10→7→8→12→16→18→19→20→21 (10.5 weeks)

Event	Slack
2	0
3	0
4	0
5	.5
6	0
7	0
8	0
9	5
10	0
11	6.5
12	0
13	7
14	0.5
15	0.5
16	0
17	3
18	0
19	0
20	0

13. Let x_t = number of nurses who will begin work in period t.

Minimize $\sum_{t=1}^{6} x_t$

subject to

$$x_1 + x_6 \geq 7$$

$$x_1 + x_2 \geq 15$$

$$x_2 + x_3 \geq 23$$

$$x_3 + x_4 \geq 29$$

$$x_4 + x_5 \geq 14$$

$$x_5 + x_6 \geq 19$$

$$x_t = 0, 1, 2, 3,\ldots \qquad \text{for } t=1, 2, 3, 4, 5, 6.$$

14. Observe that because of shifts 3 and 4, the additional time periods 5, 6, and 7 are required. The incidence table is as follows:

	Time Period	Required Drivers	Shift 1	2	3	4	5	6	7	8
1	5:00–8:30	50	1	1	0	0	0	0	0	0
2	8:30–9:00	55	0	1	0	0	0	0	0	0
3	9:00–9:30	30	0	0	1	1	0	0	0	0
4	9:30–10:00	25	1	0	1	1	0	0	0	0
5	10:00–11:00	25	1	1	1	1	0	0	0	0
6	11:00–11:30	25	1	1	1	0	0	0	0	0
7	11:30–12:00	25	1	1	0	0	0	0	0	0
8	12:00–12:30	25	1	1	0	1	0	0	0	0
9	12:30–1:00	20	1	1	1	1	0	0	0	0
10	1:00–1:30	25	1	1	1	1	1	1	0	0
11	1:30–2:00	30	1	1	1	1	1	1	0	0
12	2:00–4:30	35	0	0	1	1	1	1	0	0
13	4:30–5:00	55	0	0	1	1	0	1	0	0
14	5:00–5:30	60	0	0	1	1	0	0	1	1
15	5:30–6:00	60	0	0	1	1	1	0	1	1
16	6:00–8:30	40	0	0	0	0	1	1	1	1
17	8:30–9:00	20	0	0	0	0	1	1	0	1
18	9:00–9:30	15	0	0	0	0	1	1	0	0
19	9:30–10:00	10	0	0	0	0	1	1	1	0
20	10:00–2:00	5	0	0	0	0	0	0	1	1

14. (cont.)

Let x_j = number of drivers starting work on shift j.

Minimize $250x_1 + 250x_2 + 200x_3 + 200x_4 + 275x_5 + 275x_6 + 300x_7 + 300x_8$

subject to

$$x_1 + x_2 \geq 50$$
$$x_2 \geq 55$$
$$x_3 + x_4 \geq 30$$
$$x_1 + x_3 + x_4 \geq 25$$
$$x_1 + x_2 + x_3 + x_4 \geq 25$$
$$x_1 + x_2 + x_3 \geq 25$$
$$x_1 + x_2 \geq 25$$
$$x_1 + x_2 + x_4 \geq 25$$
$$x_1 + x_2 + x_3 + x_4 \geq 20$$
$$x_1 + x_2 + x_3 + x_4 + x_5 + x_6 \geq 25$$
$$x_1 + x_2 + x_3 + x_4 + x_5 + x_6 \geq 30$$
$$x_3 + x_4 + x_5 + x_6 \geq 35$$
$$x_3 + x_4 + x_6 \geq 55$$
$$x_3 + x_4 + x_7 + x_8 \geq 60$$
$$x_3 + x_4 + x_5 + x_7 + x_8 \geq 60$$
$$x_5 + x_6 + x_7 + x_8 \geq 40$$
$$x_5 + x_6 + x_8 \geq 20$$
$$x_5 + x_6 \geq 15$$
$$x_5 + x_6 + x_7 \geq 10$$
$$x_7 + x_8 \geq 5$$

$x_j = 0, 1, 2,\ldots$ \hspace{3cm} $j=1, 2, 3,\ldots,8$

15(a).   Using the nearest neighborn technique, the following paths are
         obtained at each iteration:

Iteration	Selection
1	4→1
2	1→2
3	5→4
4	3→5
5	2→3

Hence, the suggested path is 1→2→3→5→4→1, that is:
St. Louis→Chicago→Denver→Dallas→Memphis→St. Louis.

The total distance travelled is 285 + 1014 + 785 + 472 + 277
= 2833 miles.

15(b).   There are 4!=24 possible combinations and each needs to be considered.
         Let each city be represented by symbols.

St. Louis: S
Chicago: C
Denver: V
Memphis: M
Dallas: D

Then the following routes need to be considered:

	Route	Distance
1	S→C→V→M→D→S	3,460
2	S→C→V→D→M→S	2,833
3	S→C→M→V→D→S	3,290
4	S→C→M→D→V→S	2,924
5	S→V→M→C→D→S	4,007
6	S→V→M→D→C→S	3,582
7	S→D→C→V→M→S	3,916
8	S→D→C→M→V→S	4,007
9	S→D→V→C→M→S	3,258
10	S→D→V→M→C→S	3,290
11	S→V→D→C→M→S	3,380
12	S→V→D→M→C→S	2,924
13	S→V→C→D→M→S	3,550
14	S→V→C→M→D→S	3,519
15	S→C→D→M→V→S	3,582
16	S→C→D→V→M→S	3,321
17	S→D→M→C→V→S	3,519
18	S→D→M→V→C→S	3,460
19	S→M→D→C→V→S	3,550
20	S→M→D→V→C→S	2,833
21	S→M→V→D→C→S	3,321
22	S→M→V→C→D→S	3,916
23	S→M→C→V→D→S	3,258
24	S→M→C→D→V→S	3,380

15(b). (cont.)

Hence there are two optimal routes:

(1) St. Louis→Chicago→Denver→Dallas→Memphis→St. Louis
(2) St. Louis→Memphis→Dallas→Denver→Chicago→St. Louis

Each of these routes has a minimum distance of 2,833 miles. The result agrees with that obtained in part (a).

16. This can be solved using the nearest neighbor heuristic.

Iteration	Selection
1	2→4
2	4→5
3	5→1
4	1→3
5	3→2

Hence the sequence for processing the jobs that minimizes the total set-up time is:

1→3→2→4→5→1

This gives a total time of:

5 + 7 + 1 + 2 + 3 = 18 units.

17. Since the car must go from the bank (node 7) to the garage (node 1), we make that first decision and then proceed with the nearest neighbor heuristic.

Iteration	Path	
1	7→1	7
2	5→7	1
3	1→4	5
4	4→3	6
5	3→6	9
6	6→2	10
7	2→5	12

Hence the scheduled path is 1,→4,→3,→6,→2,→5,→7,→1

The total distance travelled is 5 + 6 + 9 + 10 + 12 + 1 + 7 = 50 miles.

18(a).

Rotation	Flights	Cost	
1	1,7	$500(2) + (125)(1.5) + 500(2)$	$= \$2187.50$
2	8,3	$500(2) + (125)(2.5) + 500(2)$	$= \$2312.50$
3	4,5	$500(2) + (125)(2) + 500(4)$	$= \$3250.00$
4	6,2	$500(1) + (125)(2) + 500(1.5)$	$= \$1500.00$
5	1	$500(2)$	$= \$1000.00$
6	2	$500(1.5)$	$= \$\ 750.00$
7	3	$500(2)$	$= \$1000.00$
8	4	$500(2)$	$= \$1000.00$
9	5	$500(4)$	$= \$2000.00$
10	6	$500(1)$	$= \$\ 500.00$
11	7	$500(2)$	$= \$1000.00$
12	8	$500(2)$	$= \$1000.00$
13	1,6	$500(2) + 125(1) + 500(1)$	$= \$1625.00$
14	6,5	$500(1) + 125(3) + 500(4)$	$= \$2875.00$
15	8,3,5	$500(2) + 125(2.5) + 500(2) + 125(.5) + 500(4)$	$= \$4375.00$
16	8,2	$500(2) + 125(4) + 500(1.5)$	$= \$2250.00$
17	3,5	$500(2) + 125(0.5) + 500(4)$	$= \$3062.50$
18	8,5	$500(2) + 125(5) + 500(4)$	$= \$3625.00$

18(b).

	1	2	3	4	5	6	7	8	9	10	11	12	13	14	15	16	17	18
1	1	0	0	0	1	0	0	0	0	0	0	0	1	0	0	0	0	0
2	0	0	0	1	0	1	0	0	0	0	0	0	0	0	0	1	0	0
3	0	1	0	0	0	0	1	0	0	0	0	0	0	0	1	0	1	0
4	0	0	1	0	0	0	0	1	0	0	0	0	0	0	0	0	0	0
5	0	0	1	0	0	0	0	0	1	0	0	0	0	1	1	0	1	1
6	0	0	0	1	0	0	0	0	0	1	0	0	1	1	0	0	0	0
7	1	0	0	0	0	0	0	0	0	0	1	0	0	0	0	0	0	0
8	0	1	0	0	0	0	0	0	0	0	0	1	0	0	1	1	0	1

Minimize $2187.50y_1 + 2312.50y_2 + 3250y_3 + 1500y_4 + 1000y_5 + 750y_6$

$+ 1000y_7 + 1000y_8 + 2000y_9 + 500y_{10} + 1000y_{11} + 1000y_{12}$

$+ 1625y_{13} + 2875y_{14} + 4375y_{15} + 2250y_{16} + 3062.50y_{17} + 3625y_{18}$

18(b) cont.

subject to

$$y_1 + y_5 + y_{13} = 1$$

$$y_4 + y_6 + y_{16} = 1$$

$$y_2 + y_7 + y_{15} + y_{17} = 1$$

$$y_3 + y_8 = 1$$

$$y_3 + y_9 + y_{14} + y_{15} + y_{17} + y_{18} = 1$$

$$y_4 + y_{10} + y_{13} + y_{14} = 1$$

$$y_1 + y_{11} = 1$$

$$y_2 + y_{12} + y_{15} + y_{16} + y_{18} = 1$$

$$y_i = 0,1 \qquad \text{for } i=1, 2,\ldots,18$$

19(a).

Tables 1 and 2 are constructed below to give the availability and requirements of aircraft by city and time of the day.

	Supply Points			Demand Points	
	Location	Availability		Location	Requirement
1	New York	11:00 a.m.	1	Chicago	9:00 a.m.
2	Denver	4:30 p.m.	2	St. Louis	3:00 p.m.
3	Phoenix	3:30 p.m.	3	Denver	1:30 p.m.
4	Phoenix	2:00 p.m.	4	St. Louis	12:00 noon
5	New York	8:00 p.m.	5	Phoenix	4:00 p.m.
6	St. Louis	1:00 p.m.	6	New York	12:00 noon
7	Chicago	2:30 p.m.	7	New York	12:30 p.m.
8	Denver	11:00 a.m.	8	Chicago	9:00 a.m.
9	Chicago	12:00 midnight(a.m.)	9	Chicago	12:00 midnight
10	Chicago	12:00 midnight(a.m.)	10	Chicago	12:00 midnight
11	New York	12:00 midnight(a.m.)	11	New York	12:00 midnight
12	New York	12:00 midnight(a.m.)	12	New York	12:00 midnight

19a (cont.)

The cost table can now be constructed and is shown in Table 3 below.

	1	2	3	4	5	6	7	8	9	10	11	12
1	∞	900	∞	∞	2700	0	0	∞	1500	1500	0	0
2	∞	∞	∞	∞	∞	∞	∞	∞	1500	1500	1800	1800
3	∞	∞	∞	∞	0	∞	∞	∞	1800	1800	2700	2700
4	∞	∞	∞	∞	0	∞	∞	∞	1800	1800	2700	2700
5	∞	∞	∞	∞	∞	∞	∞	∞	1500	1500	0	0
6	∞	0	∞	∞	1500	∞	∞	∞	600	600	900	900
7	∞	∞	∞	∞	∞	∞	∞	∞	0	0	1500	1500
8	∞	1200	0	∞	1500	∞	∞	∞	1500	1500	1800	1800
9	0	600	1500	600	1800	1500	1500	0	0	0	1500	1500
10	0	600	1500	600	1800	1500	1500	0	0	0	1500	1500
11	1500	900	1800	900	2700	0	0	1500	1500	1500	0	0
12	1500	900	1800	900	2700	0	0	1500	1500	1500	0	0

Table 3. Cost Table (C_{ij})

19(b).

Assignment Model

Let $x_{ij} = $ 1   If the aircraft at "supply point" i is assigned to "requirement" j.

             0   If not.

$$\text{Minimize} \quad \sum_{i=1}^{12} \sum_{i=1}^{12} c_{ij} x_{ij}$$

subject to

$$\sum_{i=1}^{12} x_{ij} = 1 \qquad j=1, 2, \ldots, 12$$

$$\sum_{j=1}^{12} x_{ij} = 1 \qquad i=1, 2, \ldots, 12$$

$$x_{ij} = 0,1 \qquad \text{for } i,j=1, 2, \ldots, 12.$$

Chapter 8

1. (a) $U_{100} = 4878$ $\ell_1 = 5$

   R = 4878 − 5 = 4873 hours

   (b)

Mid point (x_i)	Life of bulbs (in hours)	Tally marks	Frequency (# of bulbs)	c.f.
250	0- 500	𝖄𝖎 𝖓𝖎 𝖙𝖍𝖎 𝖙𝖍𝖎 𝖉𝖍𝖎 𝖙𝖓 𝖙𝖓 𝖙𝖓 (!!	43	43
750	500-1000	𝖓𝖎 𝖓𝖚 𝖓𝖎 𝖓𝖎 𝖎𝖎𝖎	24	67
1250	1000-1500	𝖓𝖎 𝖓𝖎 𝖎𝖎𝖎	14	81
1750	1500-2000	𝖓𝖎 𝖎𝖎𝖎	9	90
2250	2000-2500	𝖎𝖎𝖎	3	93
2750	2500-3000	𝖎𝖎𝖎	3	96
3250	3000-3500	𝖎𝖎	2	98
3750	3500-4000	𝖎	1	99
4250	4000-4500		0	99
4750	4500-5000	𝖎	1	100

2. Mean = m = $\dfrac{\Sigma f_i x_i}{N}$ = $\dfrac{92000}{100}$ = 920 hours

Median = md = $500 + \dfrac{500}{24}$ (50 − 43) = 500 + 145.833 = 645.833 hours

Mode = 250 hours

   1st Quartile = $0 + \dfrac{500}{43}$ (25 − 0) = 290.698 hours

   3rd Quartile = $1000 + \dfrac{500}{14}$ (75 − 67) = 1285.714 hours

Mean deviation = $\dfrac{1}{N} \sum_{i=1}^{n} f_i (|x_i - m|)$ = $\dfrac{1}{100}$ 65780 = 657.80 hours

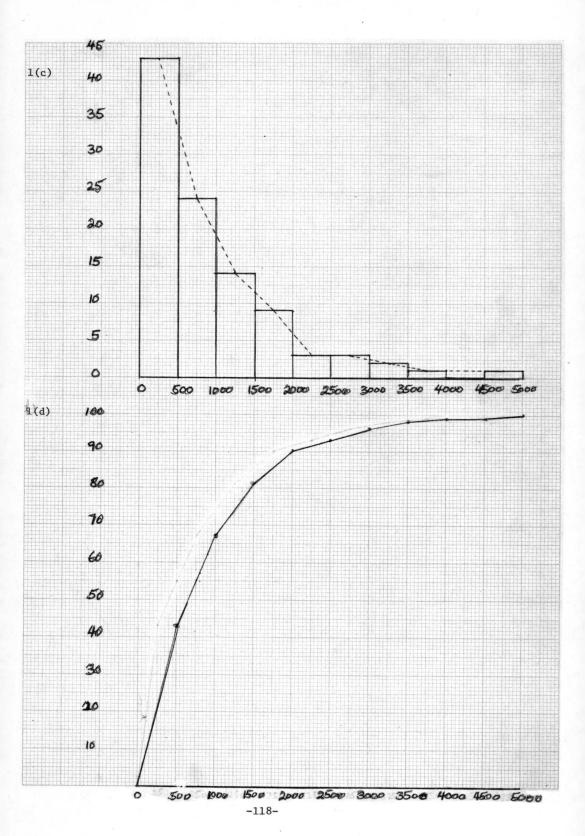

1(c)

1(d)

$$\text{Variance} = \frac{1}{N} \sum_{i=1}^{n} f_i \, x_i^2 - m^2 = \frac{1}{100} \, 161250000 - (920)^2 = 766100 \text{ (hours)}^2$$

Standard deviation = 875.2714 hours

$$\text{Coefficient of variation} = \frac{\text{standard deviation}}{\text{mean}} = \frac{875.2714}{920} = 0.9514$$

3. (a) 43%

   (b) 37.8%

   (c) 4.8%

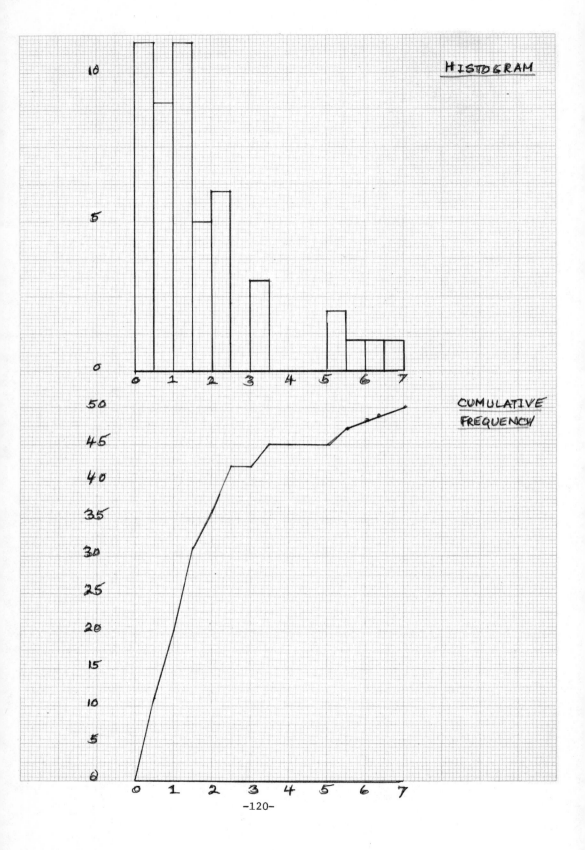

4. (a)

Mid point x_i	Holding time (in Min. & Sec).	Tally Marks	Frequency (# calls) f_i	c.f.
0:15	0:00 – 0:30	N N l	11	11
0:45	0:30 – 1:00	N llll	9	20
1:15	1:00 – 1:30	N Nl l	11	31
1:45	1:30 – 2:00	N	5	36
2:15	2:00 – 2:30	N l	6	42
2:45	2:30 – 3:00		0	42
3:15	3:00 – 3:30	lll	3	45
3:45	3:30 – 4:00		0	45
4:45	4:30 – 5:00		0	45
5:15	5:00 – 5:30	ll	2	47
5:45	5:30 – 6:00	l	1	48
6:15	6:00 – 6:30	l	1	49
6:45	6:30 – 7:00	l	1	50

5. Mean = $m = \dfrac{\Sigma f_i x_i}{\Sigma f_i} = \dfrac{85:30}{50} = 1:41.4 = 1.69$ min.

Variance = $\dfrac{1}{N} \displaystyle\sum_{i=1}^{n} f_i x_i^2 - m^2 = \dfrac{273.125}{50} - (1.69)^2 = 2.6064 \ (\text{min})^2$

Standard deviation = 1.6144 min. = 1:36.9

The percentage holding times that lie within a range of (mean $\pm$ standard deviation) is 83% (83.2%).

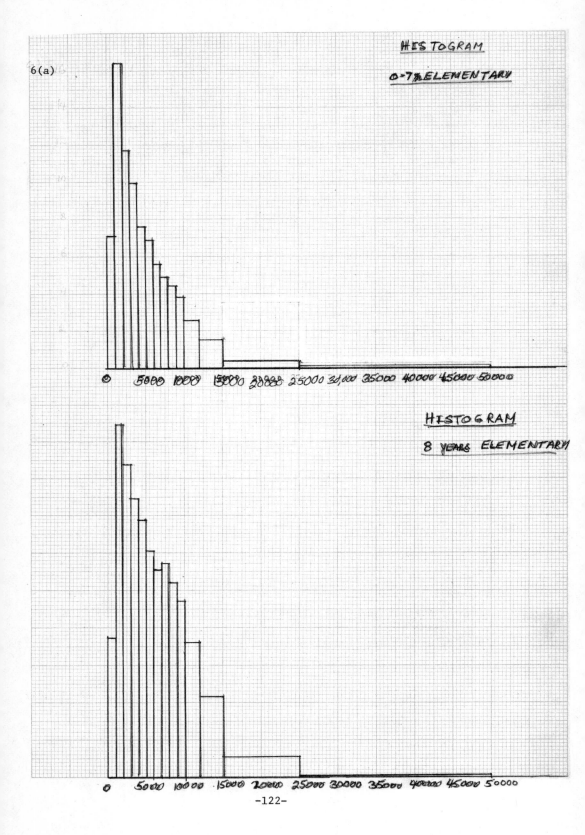

6(a)

HISTOGRAM

0-7½ ELEMENTARY

0   5000 10000 15000 20000 25000 30,000 35000 40000 45000 50000

HISTOGRAM

8 YEARS ELEMENTARY

0   5000 10000 15000 20000 25000 30000 35000 40000 45000 50000

6(a)

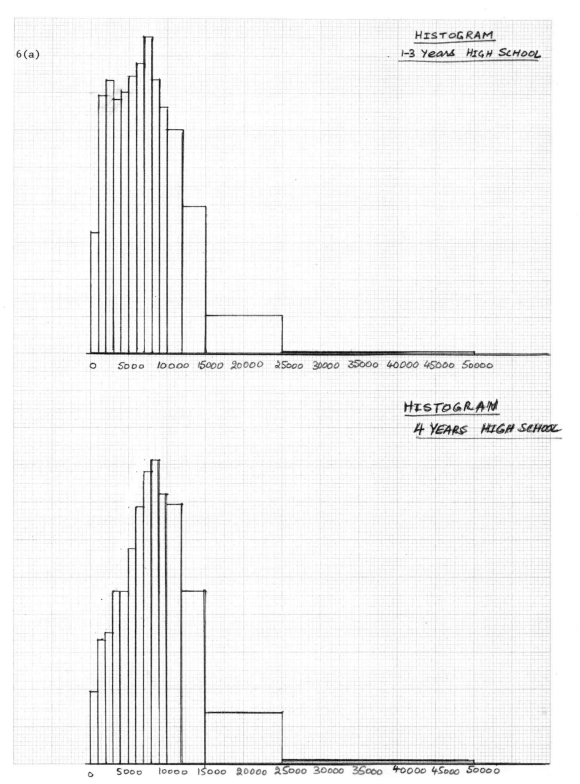

0   5000   10000   15000   20000   25000   30000   35000   40000   45000   50000

0   5000   10000   15000   20000   25000   30000   35000   40000   45000   50000

6(a)

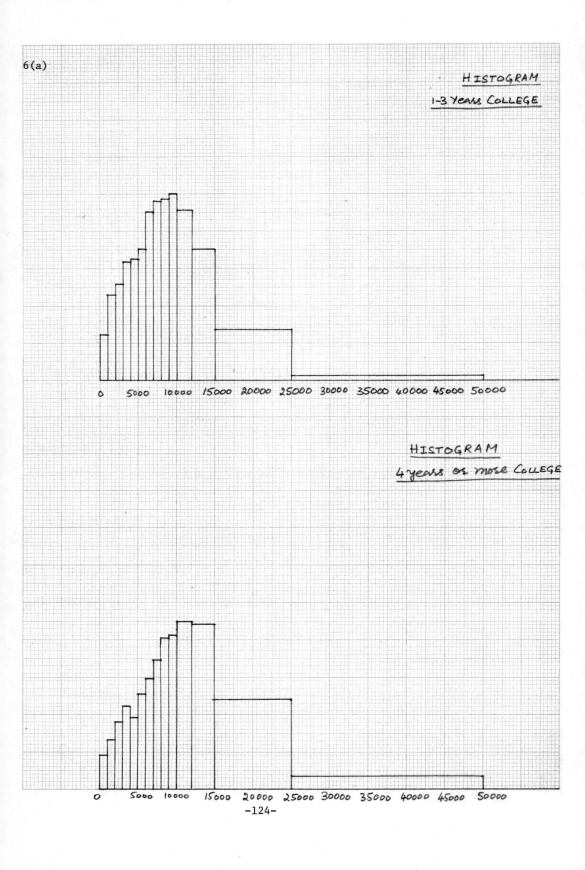

6(b)

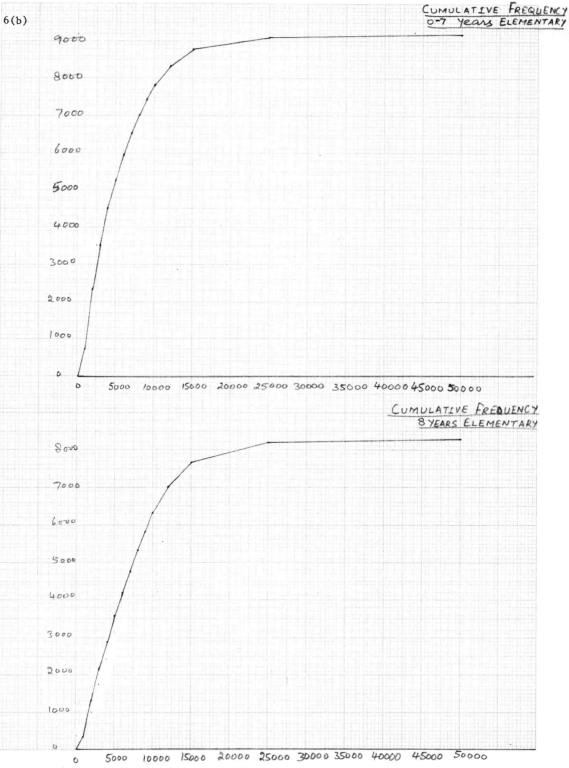

CUMULATIVE FREQUENCY
0-7 YEARS ELEMENTARY

CUMULATIVE FREQUENCY
8 YEARS ELEMENTARY

6(b)

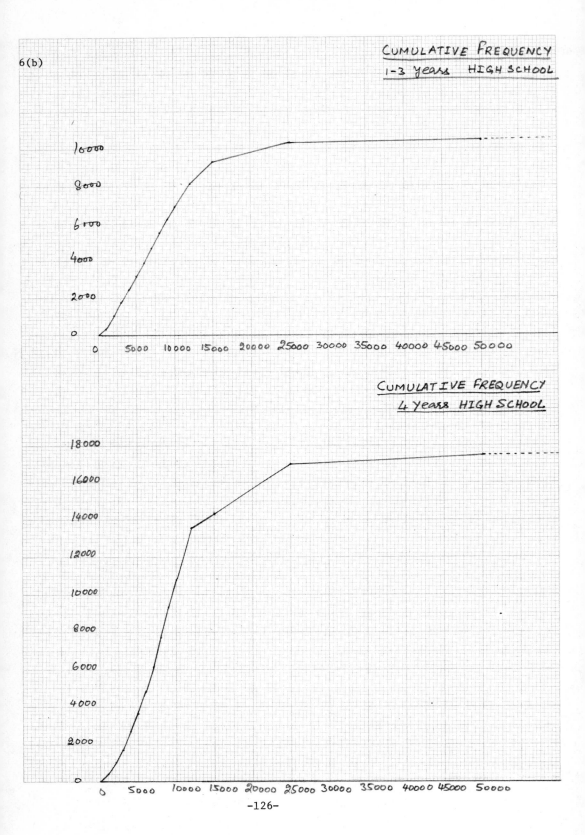

CUMULATIVE FREQUENCY
1-3 years   HIGH SCHOOL

10000

8000

6000

4000

2000

0

0   5000   10000 15000   20000 25000 30000 35000 40000 45000 50000

CUMULATIVE FREQUENCY
4 years HIGH SCHOOL

18000

16000

14000

12000

10000

8000

6000

4000

2000

0

0   5000   10000 15000   20000 25000 30000 35000 40000 45000 50000

6(b)

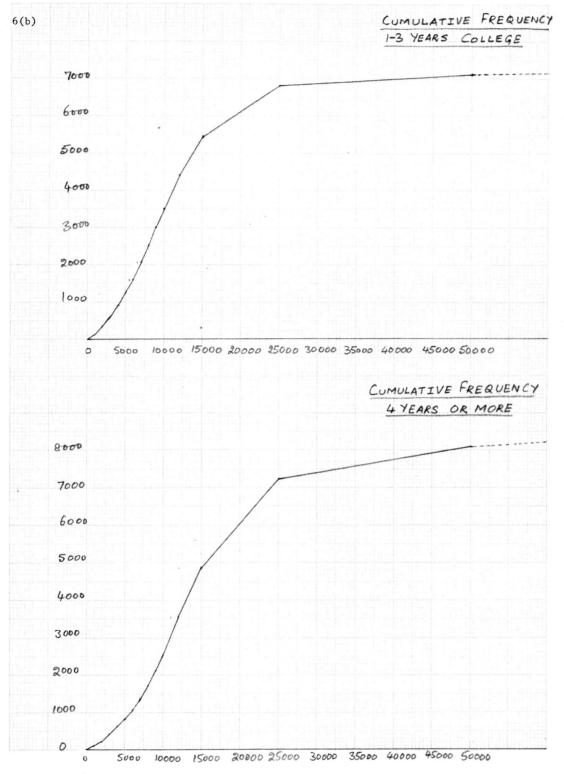

CUMULATIVE FREQUENCY
1-3 YEARS COLLEGE

CUMULATIVE FREQUENCY
4 YEARS OR MORE

6. (a) There are many ways to use the information of last income group ($50,000 and over). But we will take the mid point of last interval to be $50,000 plus half the width of last but one interval i.e., $50,000 + $12,500 = $62,500.

		Elementary		High School		College	
		0-7 yrs	8 yrs	1-3 yrs	4 yrs	1-3 yrs	4yrs or more
mean = m = $\dfrac{\Sigma f_i x_i}{\Sigma f_i = N}$		$\dfrac{51776500}{9185}$	$\dfrac{59070000}{8266}$	$\dfrac{92551000}{10506}$	$\dfrac{204077500}{19484}$	$\dfrac{85441000}{7145}$	$\dfrac{133398500}{8231}$
		$5637.07	$7146.14	$8809.35	$10474.11	$11958.15	$16206.84
median = md = $1_i + \dfrac{h}{f_i}[\dfrac{N}{2} - C]$		$4000 + \dfrac{1000}{764}(\dfrac{9185}{2} - 450)$	$5000 + \dfrac{1000}{604}(\dfrac{8266}{2} - 3583)$	$7000 + \dfrac{1000}{851}(5253 - 4664)$	$9000 + \dfrac{1000}{1445}(9742 - 9332)$	$1000 + \dfrac{2000}{908}(\dfrac{7145}{2} - 3508)$	$12000 + \dfrac{3000}{1324}(\dfrac{8231}{2} - 3519)$
		$4119.76	$5910.60	$7692.13	$9283.74	$10142.07	$13351.60

7(a)

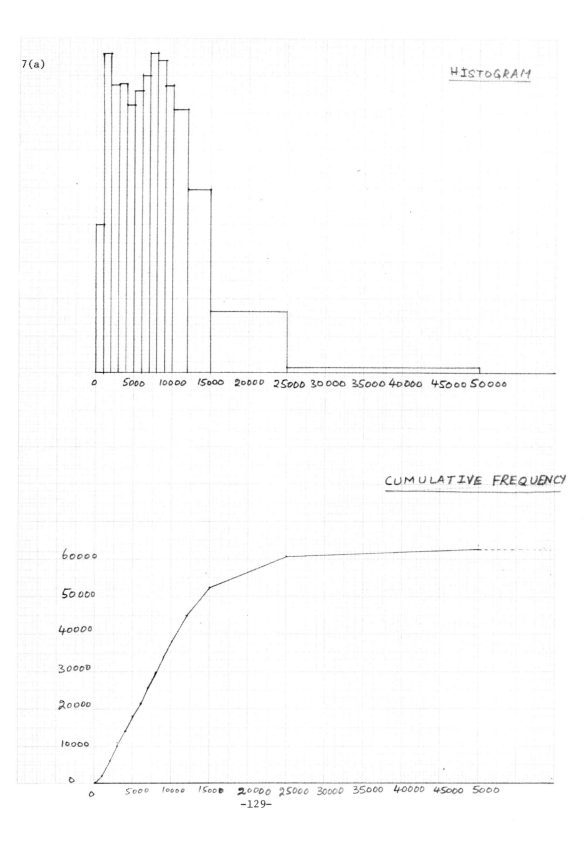

HISTOGRAM

5000 10000 15000 20000 25000 30000 35000 40000 45000 50000

CUMULATIVE FREQUENCY

60000

50000

40000

30000

20000

10000

0

0   5000   10000   15000   20000 25000 30000 35000 40000 45000 50000

7. (b) Mean = m = $\dfrac{\Sigma f_i x_i}{\Sigma f_i}$ = $\dfrac{626314500}{62817}$ = $\underline{\$9970.46}$

Variance = $\dfrac{1}{N} \Sigma_i f_i x_i^2 - (m)^2$

$= \dfrac{1}{62817} \, 10281638750000 - (m)^2$

$= 1636760550 - 99410108.86$

$= 64265946.14 \, (\$)^2$

Standard deviation = $\underline{\$8016.60}$

Median = m_d = $8000 + \dfrac{1000}{4207} (\dfrac{62817}{2} - 29775)$

$= \underline{\$8388.28}$

1st Quartile = $4000 + \dfrac{1000}{3603} (\dfrac{62817}{4} - 14074)$

$= \underline{\$4452.47}$

3rd Quartile = $12000 + \dfrac{3000}{7429} (\dfrac{(62817)3}{4} - 44948)$

$= \underline{\$12874.18}$

Sixtieth Percentile = $9000 + \dfrac{1000}{3867} (\dfrac{(62817)60}{100} - 33982)$

$= \underline{\$9958.93}$

Nintieth Percentile = $15000 + \dfrac{10000}{8431} (\dfrac{(62817)90}{100} - 52377)$

$= \underline{\$19932.16}$

8. (a) The percentage household in the mean ± standard deviation
range is

$\dfrac{100}{62817} [52377 + (17987.06 - 15,000) \dfrac{8431}{10000}] -$

$\dfrac{100}{62817} [2008 + (1953.86 - 1000) \dfrac{4299}{1000}]$

$= 87.3894 - 9.7245 = \underline{77.6649}$

8. (b) The percentage household in the mean ± 2(standard deviation) range is

$$\frac{100}{62817} \left[60808 + (26003.66 - 25,000)\frac{1794}{25000}\right] - 0$$

$$= \underline{96.9165}$$

8. (c) The percentage household in the mean ± 3(standard deviation) range is

$$\frac{100}{62817} \left[60808 + (34020.26 - 25000)\frac{1794}{25000}\right] - 0$$

$$= \underline{97.8323}$$

9. We can see in problem 6 that if we try to have class interval of equal size say 10,000, then in one of the class intervals i.e. (0-10,000) on an average more than 50% of the frequency falls. This will not help to get a good look at the data, becuase we are just including more than 50% of frequency in one interval and less than 50% in more than 5 intervals. Also we should not make more class intervals such that the class intervals are not meaning-ful. For example, dividing the class interval 0-1000 into 20 class intervals of equal size. In the light of the given range of the data, it is not interesting to use at class interval of size 50.

In order to study the data, we need to choose the appropriate size class intervals from which meaningful information can be derived.

10(a)

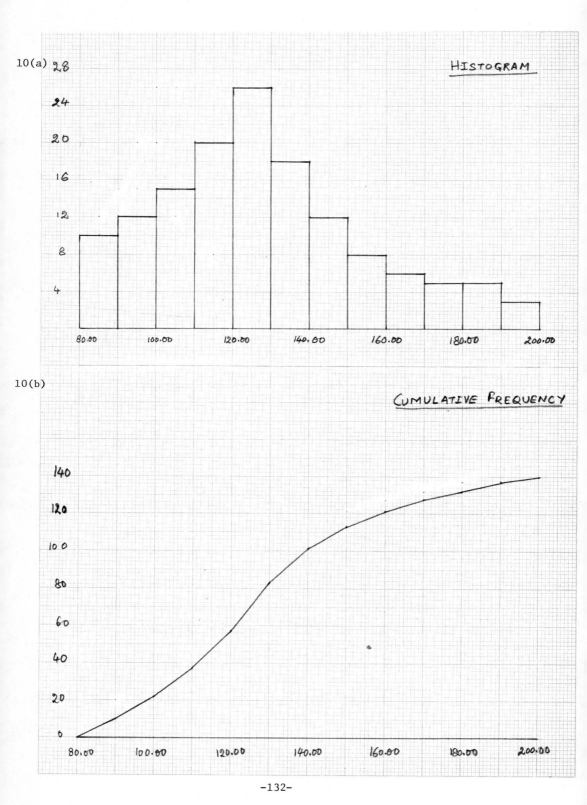

HISTOGRAM

10(b)

CUMULATIVE FREQUENCY

10.

	Mid point x_i	No. of Employees f_i	Cumulative Frequency
-60	85.00	10	10
-50	95.00	12	22
-40	105.00	15	37
-30	115.00	20	57
-20	125.00	26	83
-10	135.00	18	101
0	145.00	12	113
10	155.00	8	121
20	165.00	6	127
30	175.00	5	132
40	185.00	5	137
50	195.00	3	140

$$\text{Mean} = m = \frac{\Sigma f_i x_i}{\Sigma f_i} = \frac{17900}{140} = \$127.86$$

$$\text{Median} = m_d = 120.00 + \frac{10.00}{26} \left(\frac{140}{2} - 57\right)$$
$$= \$125.00$$

$$\text{Mode} = \$125.00$$

$$\text{Variance} = \frac{1}{N} \sum_{i=1}^{n} f_i x_i^2 - (m)^2$$
$$= 730.4082 \ (\$)^2$$

$$\text{Standard deviation} = \$27.03$$

$$\text{Coefficient of variation} = \frac{27.03}{127.86} = \underline{0.2114}$$

11. (a) Percentage of $[x \leq \bar{x}] = \frac{100}{N} \left[C + (\bar{x} - \ell) \frac{f_i}{h}\right]$

Percentage of $[x \geq \bar{x}] = 100 - \frac{100}{N} \left[c + (\bar{x} - \ell) \frac{f_i}{h}\right]$

$$= 100 - \frac{100}{140} \left[127 + (175-170)\frac{5}{10}\right]$$

$$= 100 - \frac{1}{14} \ 1295 = 100 - 92.5 = \underline{7.5}$$

(b) $\frac{100}{140} \ [57 + \frac{26}{10} \ (125.00 - 120.00)] = \underline{42.86\%}$

(c) The percentage of weekly wages in the range 127.86 ± 54.06

Percentage of $[x \leq 181.92]$ - Percentage of $[x \leq 73.8]$

$\frac{100}{140} \ [132 + (181.92 - 180)\frac{5}{10} \ ] - 0$

$\frac{100}{140} \ (0.96) = \underline{68.57}$

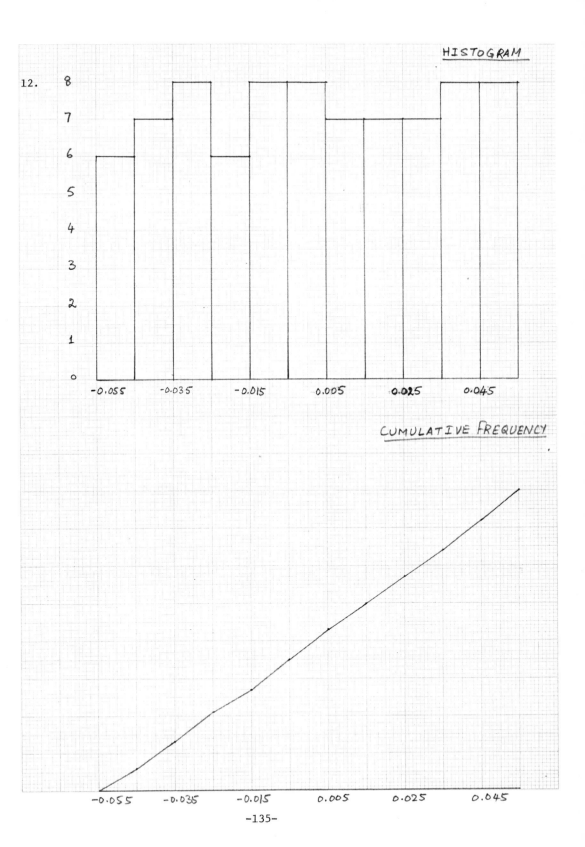

12.

HISTOGRAM

CUMULATIVE FREQUENCY

12. $Mean = m = \dfrac{\sum\limits_{i=1}^{n} f_i x_i}{\Sigma f_i} = \dfrac{.12}{80} = 0.0015$ inch

$Variance = \dfrac{1}{N} \sum\limits_{i=1}^{n} f_i x_i^2 - (m)^2$

$= \dfrac{1}{80} \; 0.0792 - (0.0015)^2$

$= 0.00099 - 0.00000225$

$= 0.00098775 \; (inch)^2$

Standard deviation = 0.03142865 inch

13.

	Percentile	Difference between successive percentile
0	−0.05	0.01
10	−0.04	0.01
20	−0.03	0.01
30	−0.02	0.01
40	−0.01	0.01
50	0.00	0.01
60	0.01	0.01
70	0.02	0.01
80	0.03	0.01
90	0.04	0.01
100	0.05	0.01

The differences are similar.

The frequency is evenly distributed.

14.   Frequency distribution

	x_i	f_i
F	0	23
S	1	37
		60

Percentage success $= \dfrac{37}{60} \times 100 = 61.67$.

15. (a)

Number of rainy days	Tally Marks	# of Weeks
0	~~NN~~ ~~NN~~ ~~NN~~ I	16
1	~~NN~~ ~~NN~~ ~~NN~~ ~~NN~~ I	21
2	~~NN~~ III	8
3	III	3
4	III	3
5	I	1
		52

15. (b) Mean $= m = \dfrac{\Sigma f_i x_i}{\Sigma f_i} = \dfrac{63}{52} = 1.212$ days

Variance $= \dfrac{1}{N} \Sigma f_i x_i^2 - (m)^2$

$= \dfrac{153}{52} - (1.212)^2 = 2.9423 - 1.468944$

$= 1.473356 \ (\text{days})^2$

Standard deviation $= 1.2138$ days

15(b)

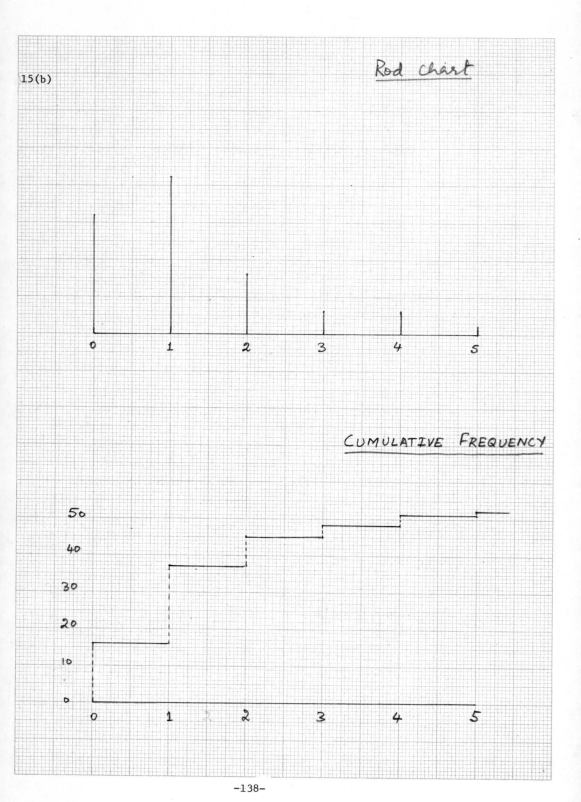

CUMULATIVE FREQUENCY

16. The possibility of rain on the day in Shine City is

$(\frac{0}{7} \quad \frac{16}{52} + \frac{1}{7} \quad \frac{21}{52} + \frac{2}{7} \quad \frac{8}{52} + \frac{3}{7} \quad \frac{3}{52} + \frac{4}{7} \quad \frac{3}{52} + \frac{5}{7} \quad \frac{1}{52})$

= .1731 (Ans.)

17. (b) Mean = $m = \dfrac{\Sigma f_i x_i}{\Sigma f_i} = \dfrac{320}{255} = 1.2549$

Variance = $\dfrac{1}{N} \Sigma f_i x_i^2 - (m)^2$

$= \dfrac{1}{255} 728 - 1.5748 = 1.2801$

Standard deviation = 1.1314

18. (a)

# of Minor defects	# of cars	c.f.	# of major defects	# of cars
0	8	8	0	35
1	17	25	1	10
2	12	37	2	3
3	7	44	3	1
4	3	47		49
5	2	49		
	49			

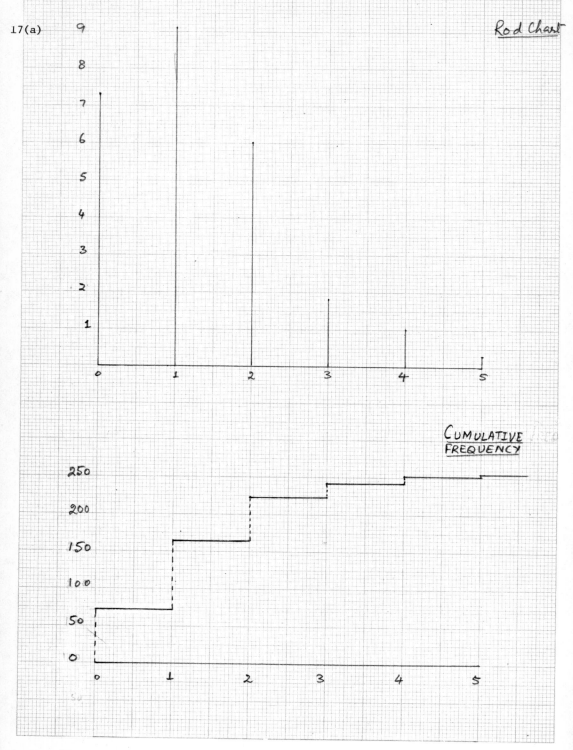

Rod Chart

CUMULATIVE
FREQUENCY

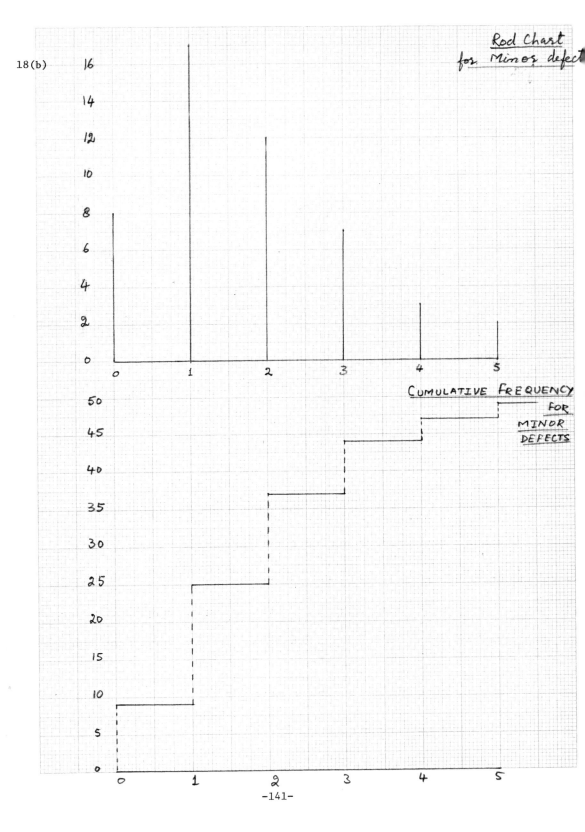

18(b)

Rod Chart for Minor defect

CUMULATIVE FREQUENCY FOR MINOR DEFECTS

18(b)

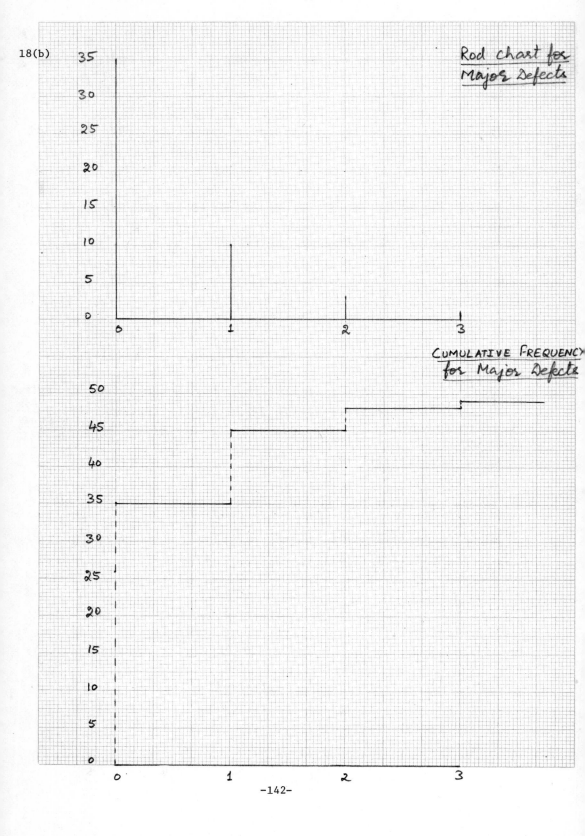

Rod chart for
Major Defects

CUMULATIVE FREQUENCY
for Major Defects

18. (c) Mean $= m_{minor} = \dfrac{\sum_i f_i x_i}{\sum_i f_i} = \dfrac{84}{49} = 1.7143$ # of defects

$\text{Variance}_{minor} = \dfrac{\sum_i f_i x_i^2}{N} - (m)^2$

$= \dfrac{1}{49} \; 226 - (m)^2 = 1.6734$

Standard deviation$_{minor}$ $= 1.2936$ # of defects

Mean $= m_{major} = \dfrac{\sum_i f_i x_i}{\sum f_i} = \dfrac{19}{49} - 0.3878$ # of defects

$\text{Variance}_{major} = \dfrac{\sum_i f_i x_i^2}{N} - (m)^2$

$= \dfrac{31}{49} - (m)^2 = .4823$

Standard deviation$_{major}$ $= 0.6945$ # of defects

19. (a)

Number of Defects	Number of cars	
0	43	43
1	27	70
2	15	85
3	8	93
4	3	96
5	2	98
	98	

19. (b) We use rod chart because the number of defects is a discrete quantity.

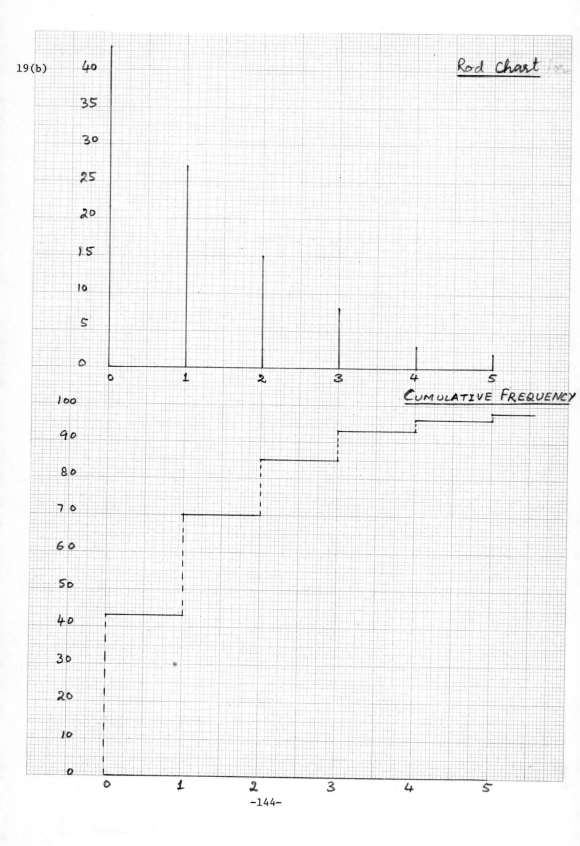

19(b)

Rod Chart

Cumulative Frequency

19. (c) Mean $= m = \dfrac{\Sigma f_i x_i}{\Sigma f_i} = \dfrac{103}{98} = 1.0510$ # of defects

$$\text{Variance} = \dfrac{\Sigma f_i x_i^2}{N} - (m)^2$$

$$= \dfrac{1}{98}\ 257 - (m)^2 = 1.5178$$

Standard deviation $= 1.2320$ # of defects.

20. (a) Mean $= m = \dfrac{\Sigma f_i x_i}{\Sigma f_i} = \dfrac{6017.3}{60} = 100.288$ gms.

$$\text{Variance} = \dfrac{\Sigma f_i x_i^2}{N} - (m)^2$$

$$= 0.213364$$

Standard deviation $= 0.4619$ gms.

(b) Mean $= m_x = u + cm_y = 100 + 10\ \dfrac{\Sigma f_i y_i}{\Sigma f_i}$

$$= 100 + 10\ \dfrac{1.73}{60} = 100.\ 2883 \text{ gms.}$$

$$\text{Variance} = (\text{Var.})_x = c^2(\text{Var})_y = (10)^2[\Sigma_i f_i y_i^2 - (m_y)^2]$$

$$= 100\ (0.00213364) = 0.213364$$

Standard deviation $= 0.4619$ gms.

The computation becomes lot more simpler after the transformation.

But in doing transformation we need extra column for y_i.

Chapter 9

1. $p = .57 \qquad n = 15$

   The probability that they will end up watching the show is

   $$\sum_{x=8}^{15} \binom{15}{x}(.57)^x(1-.57)^{15-x} = p[x \geq 8]$$

   $B[8;.60,15] = 0.7896 \geq p[x \geq 8] \geq 0.6535 = B[8;.55,15]$

   By interpolation, $p[x \geq 8] = \underline{0.7079}$ (approx.)

2. $p = 0.85 \quad q = 0.15 \quad n = 12$

   The probability that there has been at most only one accident

   caused by an error is $\displaystyle\sum_{x=0}^{1} \binom{12}{x} (0.15)^x(1-.15)^{12-x} = \underline{0.4435}$

3. $n = 30 \qquad p = .10$

   We will use Poisson tables

   $\lambda = np = 3$

   The probability that the builder will not be able to meet the

   guarantee

   $$= \sum_{x=7}^{\infty} \frac{e^{-3}\,3^x}{x!} = 1 - \sum_{x=0}^{6} \frac{e^{-3}\,3^x}{x!} = 1 - 0.966 = \underline{0.034}$$

4. $n = 50 \quad p = .01 \quad \lambda = np = .5$

   The probability that the lot will be accepted

   $$= \frac{e^{-.5}(.5)^0}{0!} = \underline{0.607}$$

5. $n = 50 \qquad p = 0.01 \qquad \lambda = np = .5$

   The probability that the lot will be accepted

   $$= \frac{e^{-.5}(.5)^0}{0!} + \frac{e^{-.5}(.5)^1}{1!} \quad \frac{e^{-.5}(.5)^0}{0!}$$

   $$= 0.607 + (0.303)(0.607) = \underline{0.7909}$$

6. $n = 2000 \qquad p = .0008 \qquad \lambda = np = 1.6$

The probability that more than four individuals will suffer from

adverse reactions

$$= \sum_{x=5}^{\infty} \frac{e^{-1.6}(1.6)^x}{x!} = 1 - \sum_{x=0}^{4} \frac{e^{-1.6}(1.6)^x}{x!} = 1 - 0.976 = \underline{0.024}$$

7. $n = 42 \qquad p = \frac{2}{45} \qquad \lambda = \frac{28}{15} = 1.87$

The probability of getting three or more effective cases out of 42

$$\sum_{x=3}^{\infty} \frac{e^{-1.87}(1.87)^x}{x!} = 1 - \sum_{x=0}^{2} \frac{e^{-1.87}(1.87)^x}{x!} = 1 - 0.712 = \underline{0.288}$$

8. (a) The probability that only a single test will be needed is

$(1 - 0.01)^{10} = \underline{0.0944}$

(b) The mean number of tests

$= 1 (0.99)^6 + 7 (1 - (0.99)^6)$

$= .94148 + 7 (.05852) = \underline{1.35112 \text{ tests}}$

9. $\lambda = 8 \qquad \sum_{x=0}^{n} \frac{8^x e^{-8}}{x!} \geq .99$

By using Tables, $\underline{n = 15}$

We assume that the arrival of the customers is independent and is

not dependent on the previous arrival.

10. Since the demand rate is uniformly spread over the entire day, the

demand for 5 hours is $5 \cdot \frac{8}{14} = \frac{20}{7}$

The probability that the store will run out of the item by that

time

$$= \sum_{x=6}^{\infty} \frac{e^{-20/7}(20/7)^x}{x!} = 1 - \sum_{x=0}^{5} \frac{e^{-20/7}(20/7)^x}{x!} = 1 - 0.929 = \underline{0.071}$$

11. Expected number of responses $= 430 \cdot \frac{45}{100} = 193.5$

The probability that at least 200 will respond

$$\sum_{x=200}^{430} \binom{430}{x} (.45)^x (.55)^{430-x}.$$

12. p = .15

The probability that the eighth caller wins the prize is

$(.85)^7(.15)$

The probability that the prize goes to any one of the first five callers

$$= \sum_{x=1}^{5} (.85)^{x-1}(.15) = .15\frac{(1-(.85)^5)}{1-.85} = 1 - (.85)^5 = \underline{0.5563}$$

The mean number of callers needed to get a winner is $\frac{1}{.15} = \frac{20}{3} = \underline{6\ 2/3}$

13. The probability that the switch will fail any time after 500 trials is

$$\sum_{x=0}^{\infty} (1-.002)^{500+x}.002 = (1-.002)^{500}(.002)\frac{1}{(.002)} = (1-.002)^{500} = \underline{0.3675}$$

The probability that the switch will fail on or before 300 trials is

$$\sum_{x=1}^{300} (.002)(1-.002)^{x-1} = (.002)\frac{[1-(.998)^{300}]}{1-.998} = 1-(.998)^{300}$$

$$= \underline{0.4515}$$

14. The probability that an arriving job will be forced to wait for a second chance

$$= 1 - \int_0^{100} \frac{1}{155} e^{-1/155\ x} dx = 1 - (1 - e^{-100/155}) = e^{-20/31}$$

$$= 0.5346.$$

The expected number of jobs to finish within the first quantum

$$= 750 \left(\int_0^{100} \frac{1}{155} e^{-1/155x} dx\right) = 750(1 - e^{-100/155}) = 750(1 - e^{-20/31})$$

$$= 750(.4754) = 356.55$$

15. The probability that he would have started work on Hurry's car by

9:30 A.M.

$$= \int_0^{30} \frac{1}{30} e^{-1/30x} \, dx = 1 - e^{-30/30} = \underline{0.6321}$$

The probability that the mechanic would still be working on

the first car is $e^{-45/30} = e^{-1.5} = \underline{0.2231}$

16. $\lambda = 16$ cars repaired per day

The probability that he has to work overtime beyond the eight

hours he works

$$= 1 - \sum_{x=20}^{\infty} \frac{e^{-16}(16)^x}{x!} = \sum_{x=0}^{19} \frac{e^{-16}(16)^x}{x!} = \underline{0.812}$$

17. Demand $d \sim N(57,500, 8750)$

The minimum expected sale $\dfrac{\$150 \text{ million}}{\$3750} = 40,000$ cars

The probability that the company will not be able to realize

an income of that magnitude is $p[d < 40,000]$

$$= p\left[z = \frac{d - 57,500}{8750} < \frac{40,000 - 57,500}{8750}\right]$$

$$= p[z < -2] = 1 - .9722 = \underline{0.0228}$$

18. (a) The probability that a tube will be burnt out in 6500 hours

is $p[x < 6500] = p\left[z = \dfrac{x - 7500}{500} < \dfrac{6500 - 7500}{500}\right]$

$= p[z < -2] = 0.0228$

The probability that replacement of the tubes will be needed before

6500 hours is $\displaystyle\sum_{x=5}^{12} \binom{12}{x} (0.0228)^x (.9772)^{12-x}$

$$= 1 - \sum_{x=0}^{4} \binom{12}{x} (0.0228)^x (.9772)^{12-x}$$

$= 1 - 0.9998 \text{ (approx)}$

$= \underline{0.0002}$

18. (b) The probability that a tube will be burnt out in 7000

hours is $p[x<7000] = p[z = \frac{x-7500}{500} < \frac{7000-7500}{500}]$

$= p[z<-1] = 1 - 0.8413 = 0.1583$

The probability that replacement of the tubes will be needed

before 700 hours is $\sum_{x=5}^{12} \binom{12}{x} (0.1583)^x (0.8413)^{12-x}$

$= 1 - 0.9670 = \underline{0.033}$

18. (c) The probability that a tube will be burnt out in 7500 hours is

$p[x<7500] = p[z = \frac{x-7500}{500} < \frac{7500-7500}{500}] = p[z<0] = 0.5$

The probability that replace of the tube will be needed before

7500 hours is

$\sum_{x=5}^{12} \binom{12}{x} (1/2)^x (1/2)^{12-x}$

$= 1 - 0.1938 = \underline{0.8062}$

18. (d) The probability that a tube will be burnt out in 8000 hours is

$p[x<8000] = p[z = \frac{x-7500}{500} < \frac{8000-7500}{500}] = p[z<1] = 0.8413$

The probability that replacement of the tube will be needed

before 8000 hours is $\sum_{x=5}^{12} \binom{12}{x} (0.8413)^x (0.1583)^{12-x}$

$\sum_{x=0}^{7} \binom{12}{x} (0.1583)^x (0.8413)^{12-x} = \underline{0.9998}$

19. $\lambda = \frac{\Sigma f_i x_i}{\Sigma f_i} = \frac{258}{60} = 4.3$

Number of Accidents	p_x	e_x	0_x	$\dfrac{(0_x - e_x)^2}{e_x}$
0	0.014	0.84 ⎫		
1	0.059	3.54 ⎬ 11.94 12		0.0003
2	0.126	7.56 ⎭		
3	0.180	10.80	12	0.1333
4	0.193	11.58	13	0.1741
5	0.166	9.96	9	0.0925
6	0.119	7.14	5	0.6414
7	0.073	4.38 ⎫		
8	0.039	2.34		
9	0.019	1.14 ⎬ 8.58 9		0.2056
10	0.008	0.48		
11	0.003	0.18		
12	0.001	0.06 ⎭		
		60.00		$z_m = 1.2472$

$r = 1 \qquad k = 6 \qquad m = 6 - 1 - 1 = 4$

α	.50	.25	.10	.05	.025	.01	.005
z	3.36	5.39	7.78	9.49	11.1	13.3	14.9

Clearly the obtained value of z_m is in the acceptable range.

20. If we look at the data, the frequency is more in the middle and as we go to the ends it decreases. So we will use the normal model.

   Mean and variance are the parameter for this distribution.

   Mean = m = 0.6254008 inches

   Variance = 0.00000036 $(inches)^2$

21. The probability model to be used is an exponential model.

   $$\frac{1}{\hat{\lambda}} = \frac{1}{920}$$

   The exponential model for the data is

   $$f(x) = \frac{1}{920} \, e^{-1/920x} \; ; \; x > 0.$$

Interval	p_x	e_x	0_x	$\dfrac{(e_x - 0_x)^2}{e_x}$
0- 500	0.42	42	43	0.02381
500-1000	0.24	24	24	0.00000
1000-1500	0.14	14	14	0.00000
1500-2000	0.08	8	9	0.12500
2000-2500	0.05	5	3	0.40000
2500-3000	0.03	3		
3000-3500	0.02	2		
3500-4000	0.01	1	7	0.00000
4000-4500	0.01	1	$z_m = 0.94881$	
4500-5000	0.00	0		

   (rows 2500-3000 through 4500-5000, the e_x values 3,2,1,1,0 are braced together summing to 7; $0_x = 7$)

   r = 1   k = 6   m = 6 - 1 - 1 = 4

α	.50	.25	.10	.05	.025	0.01	0.005
z	3.36	5.39	7.78	9.49	11.1	13.3	14.9

Clearly the obtained value of z_m is in the acceptable range.

22. The probability model to be used is an exponential model.

$$\frac{1}{\hat\lambda} = \frac{1}{1.69}$$

The exponential model for the data is

$$f(x) = \frac{1}{1.69} \, e^{-1/1.69x} \; ; \; x > 0$$

Interval	p_x	e_x	o_x	$\dfrac{(e_x - o_x)^2}{e_x}$
0-0.5	0.26	13.0	11	0.3077
0.5-1.0	0.19	9.5	9	0.0263
1.0-1.5	0.14	7.0	11	2.2857
1.5-2.0	0.11	5.5 ⎫ 9.5	11	0.2368
2.0-2.5	0.08	4.0 ⎭		
2.5-3.0	0.06	3.0 ⎫ 5.0	3	0.8000
3.0-3.5	0.04	2.0 ⎭		
3.5-4.0	0.03	1.5		
4.0-4.5	0.02	1.0 ⎫		
4.5-5.0	0.02	1.0 ⎪ 5.5	5	0.0455
5.0-5.5	0.01	0.5 ⎪		
5.5-6.0	0.01	0.5 ⎬		
6.0-6.5	0.01	0.5 ⎪		
6.5-7.0	0.01	0.5 ⎭		

$$z_m = 3.702$$

$$r = 1 \qquad k = 6$$

$$m = 6 - 1 - 1 = 4$$

α	.50	.25	.10	.05	0.025	0.01	0.005
z	3.36	5.39	7.78	9.49	11.1	13.3	14.9

For the obtained value of z_m, α_{z_m} lies between .50 and .25 and is not very small. In view of this we may conclude that the exponential model with $\hat\lambda = 1.69$ min is a good fit for the data.

23. Normal probability models are appropriate for the income data of
households whose heads have high school of college education.

24. The probability model which should be used is uniform model.

x	P_x	e_x	0_x	$\dfrac{(e_x - 0_x)^2}{e_x}$
-.05	$\frac{1}{11}$	7.273	6	0.2228
-.04	$\frac{1}{11}$	7.273	7	0.0100
-.03	$\frac{1}{11}$	7.273	8	0.0727
-.02	$\frac{1}{11}$	7.273	6	0.2228
-.01	$\frac{1}{11}$	7.273	8	0.0727
00	$\frac{1}{11}$	7.273	8	0.0727
+.01	$\frac{1}{11}$	7.273	7	0.0100
+.02	$\frac{1}{11}$	7.273	7	0.0100
+.03	$\frac{1}{11}$	7.273	7	0.0100
+.04	$\frac{1}{11}$	7.273	8	0.0727
+.05	$\frac{1}{11}$	7.273	8	0.0727
			80	$z_m = 0.8491$

$r = 1 \qquad k = 11 \qquad m = 11 - 1 - 1 = 9$

α	.50	.25	.10	.05	.025	0.01	0.005
z	8.34	11.4	14.7	16.9	19.0	21.7	23.6

Clearly obtained value of z_m is in the acceptable range.

25. The probability model which should be used is the Bernoulli model.
$\hat{p}$, the estimate of the probability of success. $\hat{p} = \dfrac{37}{60}$
We use Bernoulli model because events are success or failure, i.e.,

1 or 0 and it is the appropriate model for this type of situation.

26. The probability model which should be used is the Poisson model.

$$\hat{\lambda} = \frac{\Sigma f_i\, x_i}{N} = 1.212 \text{ days/week}$$

x	P_x	e_x	0_x	$\dfrac{(e_x - 0_x)^2}{e_x}$
0.	0.298	15.5	16	0.0161
1	0.361	18.8	21	0.2574
2	0.219	11.4	8	1.0140
3	0.088	4.6 ⎫		
4	0.027	1.5 ⎬ 6.3	7	0.0778
5	0.006	0.3 ⎭		

$$z_m = 1.3653$$

r = 1   k = 4   m = 4 − 1 − 1 = 2

α	.50	.25	.10	0.05	0.025	0.01	0.005
z	1.39	2.77	4.61	5.99	7.38	9.21	10.6

Clearly obtained value of z_m is in the acceptable range.

27. The probability model which should be used is the Poisson Model.

$$\hat{\lambda} = \frac{\Sigma f_i x_i}{N} = 1.255$$

x	P_x	e_x	0_x	$\dfrac{(e_x - 0_x)^2}{e_x}$
0	.285	72.7	73	0.00124
1	.358	91.3	91	0.00099
2	.225	57.4	60	0.11777

3	.094	24.0	18	1.50000
4	.029	7.4 ⎫	13	1.56957
5	.007	1.8 ⎭ 9.2		

$$z_m = 3.18957$$

r = 1   k = 5

m = 5 − 1 − 1 = 3

α	.50	.25	.10	0.05	0.025	0.01	0.005
z	2.37	4.11	6.25	7.81	9.35	11.3	12.8

For the obtained value of z_m, α_{z_m} lies between .50 and .25 and is not very small. In view of this we may conclude that the exponential model with $\hat{\lambda} = 1.255$ is a good fit for the data.

28. The probability model which should be used is the Poisson Model

$$\hat{\lambda} = \frac{1}{N} \sum_i f_i x_i = 1.714 \quad \text{\# of defects.}$$

x	P_x	e_x	0_x	$\dfrac{(e_x - 0_x)^2}{e_x}$
0	.180	8.8	8	0.07273
1	.309	15.1	17	0.23907
2	.265	13.0	12	0.07692
3	.151	7.4 ⎫		
4	.065	3.2 ⎬ 11.7 12		0.00769
5	.022	1.1 ⎭		

$$z_m = 0.39641$$

r = 1   k = 4

m = 4 − 1 − 1 = 2

α	.50	.25	.10	0.05	0.025	0.01	0.005
z	1.39	2.77	4.61	5.99	7.38	9.21	10.6

Clearly obtained value of z_m is in the acceptable range.

29. The normal probability model should be used, because the frequency is concentrated in the middle of the data and as we go to the ends it decreases.

   The parameters for this model are mean and variance.

   mean = $\hat{\mu}$ = 100.288 gms

   variance = $\hat{\sigma}^2$ = 0.2134 $(gms)^2$

30.

Cost Interval	Mid Point x_i	Tally Marks	Frequency f_i
15.95–16.95	16.5	III	3
16.95–17.95	17.5	~~IIII~~ I	6
17.95–18.95	18.5	I	16
18.95–19.95	19.5	II	19
19.95–20.95	20.5	I	13
20.95–21.95	21.5	I	12
21.95–22.95	22.5	I	8
22.95–23.95	23.5	I	3
		N =	80

The probability model which should be used for the data is the normal probability model.

Estimates of the parameters are

Mean $\hat{\mu} = \frac{1}{N} \Sigma f_i x_i = \$19.95$

Variance $\hat{\sigma}^2 = \frac{1}{N} \sum_{i=1}^{n} (x_i - \hat{\mu})^2 = \frac{1}{N} \sum_{i=1}^{n} f_i x_i^2 - \hat{\mu}^2 = 2.8975 \ (\$)^2$

The normal probability model is used because the frequency is more in the middle and as we go to ends it decreases.

31.

Interval	Mid point x_i	Frequency 0_x	P_x	e_x	$\frac{(e_x - 0_x)^2}{e_x}$
0- 200	100	20	0.249	18.7	0.0904
200- 400	300	13	0.187	14.0	0.0714
400- 600	500	9	0.140	10.5	0.2143
600- 800	700	6	0.105	7.9	0.4570
800-1000	900	10 ⎫ 13	0.079	5.9 ⎫ 10.4	0.6500
1000-1200	1100	3 ⎭	0.060	4.5 ⎭	
1200-1400	1300	3 ⎫ 6.0	0.045	3.4 ⎫ 6.0	0.0000
1400-1600	1500	3 ⎭	0.034	2.6 ⎭	
1600-1800	1700	2 ⎫	0.025	1.9 ⎫	
1800-2000	1900	1 ⎪ 8	0.019	1.4 ⎪ 5.8	0.8345
2000-2200	2100	0 ⎬	0.014	1.1 ⎬	
2200-2400	2300	3 ⎪	0.011	0.8 ⎪	
2400-2600	2500	2 ⎭	0.008	0.6 ⎭	

$$N = 75$$

$\hat{\lambda} = \frac{1}{N} \Sigma f_i x_i = \frac{52500}{75} = 700 \qquad\qquad z_m = 2.3176$

$r = 1 \qquad\qquad k = 7 \qquad\qquad m = 7 - 1 - 1 = 5$

α	.50	.25	.10	.05	0.025	0.01	0.005
z	4.35	6.63	9.24	11.1	12.8	15.1	16.7

Clearly obtained value of z_m is in the acceptable range.

32.

Number of Crimes	Frequency	p_x	e_x	$\dfrac{(e_x - 0_x)^2}{e_x}$
0-5	0 ⎫	0.020	1.2 ⎫	
6	1 ⎬ 3	0.025	1.5 ⎬ 5.3	0.9981
7	2 ⎭	0.044	2.6 ⎭	
8	4 ⎫	0.066	4.0 ⎫	0.0043
9	5 ⎬ 9	0.087	5.2 ⎬ 9.2	
10	9	0.105	6.3	1.1571
11	8	0.114	6.8	0.2118
12	9	0.114	6.8	0.7118
13	7	0.106	6.4	0.0563
14	3	0.090	5.4	1.0667
15	5 ⎫	0.072	4.3 ⎫	0.0333
16	2 ⎬ 7	0.054	3.2 ⎬ 7.5	
17	1 ⎫	0.038	2.3 ⎫	
18	1	0.026	1.6	
19	1	0.016	1.0	
20	0 ⎬ 5	0.010	0.6 ⎬ 6.1	0.1984
21	1	0.006	0.4	
22	1 ⎭	0.003	0.2 ⎭	

$$N = 60 \qquad\qquad z_m = 4.4378$$

$$r = 1 \qquad k = 1 \qquad m = 9 - 1 - 1 = 7$$

We will use the Poisson distribution model

$$\hat{\lambda} = \frac{1}{N} \sum_{i=1}^{n} f_i x_i = \frac{720}{60} = 12 \quad \text{crimes/hour}$$

α	.50	.25	.10	0.050	0.025	0.010	0.005
z	6.35	9.04	12.0	14.1	16.0	18.5	20.3

Clearly obtained value of z_m is in the acceptable range.

$$\min_{n} \sum_{i=0}^{n} \frac{e^{-12}(12)^2}{i!} \geq 0.98$$

$$n = 20 \qquad \text{crimes}$$

Number of policemen needed = 20 x 3.5 = <u>70</u>

33. 42 policemen can handle = $\frac{42}{3.5}$ = 12 crimes

The probability of 12 or less crimes in one hour

$$\sum_{i=0}^{12} \frac{e^{-12}(12)^i}{i!} = 0.575$$

The probability that the normal performance of the city police

department is not affected by this move is

$$(0.575)^6 = \underline{0.036}$$

CHAPTER 10

1. a. Continuous
    b. Discrete
    c. Continuous
    d. Continuous
    e. Quality characteristics
    f. Quality characteristics
    g. Quality characteristics
    h. Continuous
    i. Discrete
    j. Discrete

2. S = {Cowboys win, Rams win}

    P{Cowboys win} : P{Rams win} = 2:1
    P{Cowboys win} = 2/3; P{Rams win} = 1/3.

3. P{improve} = 3/10
    P{remain} = 2/3
    p{get worse} = 1/6
          3/10 + 2/3 + 1/6 = 34/30 > 1

    Therefore, his conclusion is not consistant.

4. Sum of the numbers in each categories = 211.
    Total cases = 182.
    The difference of 29 cases occurs due to the multiple crimes
    committed by some criminals. In the terminology of events, the
    union of events is obtained by counting each element only once,
    even if they belong to more than one event. The record keeping
    procedure can be improved by specifying multiple crime cases.

5. Let A: the number of customers who bought stamps
         B: the number of customers who sent parcels or registered letters.

    A = 135
    B = 36

    $A \cap B = 19.$

    $A \cup B = A + B - A \cap B = 152.$

    P[a typical customer would buy stamps] $= \dfrac{P[A]}{P[A \cup B]} = \dfrac{135}{152}.$

6. P[the system in operation] = P[both unit in operation]
    + 2 P[one unit in operation] x P[one unit out of operation]
    $= [0.85]^2 + 2[0.85] \times [0.15]$

    = 0.9775

7. P[the traffic light will require repair]
= P[bulb will fail] + P[flasher will fail] - P[both of them fail]
= [1 - 0.95] + [1 - 0.98] - [1 - 0.95]·[1 - 0.98]
= 0.069

8. P[flasher subsystem fails]
= P[both flashers fail] = $[1 - 0.95]^2$ = 0.0025

P[bulb subsystem fails] = $[1 - 0.98]^2$ = 0.0004.

P[the traffic light will require repair]
= 0.0025 + 0.0004 - (0.0025)(0.0004)
= 0.002899

The reliability of the new system
= 1 - 0.002898 = 0.997101

9.

	No. of units	Reliability	Unit Cost
Source A:	1	0.90	$100
Source B:	2	0.9375	$ 50
Source C:	3	0.908875	$ 35

Reliability/cost   A: 0.9/100 = 0.009
                    B: 0.9375/100 = 0.009375
                    C: 0.908875/105 = 0.00866

Ans. B

10. P[none of its engines has been hit]
$= \binom{4}{4} (0.3)^0 (0.7)^4$ = 0.2401

11. $P(B|E_1) = \dfrac{P[E_1 \cap B]}{P[E_1]} = \dfrac{P[B]}{P[E_1]} = \dfrac{0.24}{0.38 + 0.24} = .387$

$P(E_1|E_2) = \dfrac{P[E_1 E_2]}{P[E_2]} = 0.$

The events E_1 and E_2 are mutually exclusive. $\Rightarrow$ Not independent

12. $\lambda = 3.5$

P[no. of accident $\geq$ 4|no. of accident $\geq$ 1]

$= \dfrac{P[\text{no. of accident} \geq 4]}{P[\text{no. of accident} \geq 1]} = \dfrac{1 - \sum\limits_{i=0}^{3} \dfrac{e^{3.5}(3.5)^i}{i!}}{1 - \dfrac{e^{-3.5}(3.5)^0}{0!}}$

-162-

12 continued

$$= \frac{0.4634}{0.969} = .47189$$

13. $P(E_G) = 90/160 = 9/16$

$P(E_A) = 10/160 = 1/16$

$P(E_R) = 60/160 = 3/8$

$P(E_G \cup E_R) = 15/16$

$P(E_G | E_G \cup E_A) = 9/10$

$P(E_G E_A) = 0$

Events E_G and E_R are mutually exclusive.

14. $P(A|B) = \frac{P(AB)}{P(B)} = \frac{9/38}{18/38} = 0.5$

$P(B|A) = \frac{P(AB)}{P(A)} = \frac{9/38}{18/38} = 0.5$

$P(A|D) = \frac{P(AD)}{P(D)} = \frac{P(\text{even and odd number})}{P(D)} = 0$

$P(B|C) = \frac{P(BC)}{P(C)} = \frac{6/38}{12/38} = 0.5$

Events A and B are not independent
Events A and D are mutually exclusive.

15. P[incorrect set-up | two out of five items are defective]

$$= \frac{P[B|A]P[A]}{P[B|A]P[A]+P[B|C]P[C]}$$

$$= \frac{\binom{5}{2}(0.3)^2(0.7)^3 \cdot (0.07)}{\binom{5}{2}(0.3)^2(0.7)^3(0.07)+\binom{5}{2}(0.05)^2(0.95)^3(0.93)} = \frac{0.0216}{0.0216 + 0.0199} = 0.520.$$

where   A: incorrect set-up
        B: two out of five items are defective
        C: correct set-up

16. P[a randomly selected person does not favor the E.R.A.] =

P[he is a Republican and does not favor the E.R.A.]
+ P[he is an independent and does not favor the E.R.A.]
+ P[he is a Democrat and does not favor the E.R.A.]
= 0.43 x 0.8 + 0.22 x 0.5 + 0.35 x 0.25
= 0.5415

16 continued

$$P[A|D] = \frac{P[D|A]P[A]}{P[D|A]P[A] + P[D|B]P[B] + P[D|C]P[C]}$$

$$= \frac{0.25 \cdot 0.35}{(0.35 \times 0.35) + (0.22 \times 0.5) + (0.43 \times 0.8)} = 0.1615$$

$P[C|D] = .709$

where A: Democratic
       B: Independent
       C: Republican
       D: Biased against E.R.A.

17. P[good risk|payment in two month]

$= \dfrac{P[\text{payment in two month}|\text{good risk}] \ P[\text{good risk}]}{P[\text{payment in two month}|\text{good risk}]P[\text{good risk}] + P[\text{payment in two month}|\text{bad risk}]P[\text{bad ri}}$

$$= \frac{0.32 \times 0.85}{0.32 \times 0.85 + .21 \times .15} = 0.896$$

18. Let ρ be the traffic intensity

P[traffic intensity is in the range 0 to 0.5|one line is busy]

$$= \frac{P[P_1|0\leq\rho<0.5] \ P[0\leq\rho<0.5]}{P[P_1|0\leq\rho<0.5]P[0\leq\rho<0.5]+P[P_1|0.5\leq\rho<1]P[0.5\leq\rho<1]+)[P_i|1\leq\rho\leq15]\times P[1\leq\rho<1.5]}$$

$$= \frac{0.22 \times 0.25}{0.22 \times 0.25 + 0.33 \times 0.45 + 0.17 \times 0.3} = 0.216$$

P[traffic intensity is in the range 0.5 to 1]

$$= \frac{0.33 \times 0.45}{0.2545} = 0.5834$$

P[traffic intensity is in the range 1 to 1.5]

$$= .2003.$$

19. Let M_i be the number of i years old machines

Expected income $= 30[M_1 + M_2 + M_3 + M_4] + 50 \times M_5$

Expected service cost $= 50(.1 \times M_1 + .2M_2 + .4M_3 + .6M_4 + .7M_5)$

when expected income > expected service cost

they can make the service contract.

20. Expected annual sales for

Toy A: $750,000 \times 0.3 + 500,000 \times 0.35 + 250,000 \times .35$
$= 510,000$.

Toy B: $600,000 \times .55 + 350,000 \times .25 + 150,000 \times .2$
$= 447,500$

Toy C: $700,000 \times 0.4 + 550,000 \times .35 + 350,000 \times .25$
$= 560,000$

Ans. Toy C.

21. Difference between expected sales and production cost of

Toy A: $510,000 - 80,000 = 430,000$

Toy B: $447,500 - 100,000 = 347,500$

Toy C: $560,000 - 160,000 = 400,000$

Ans. Toy A.

22.

		E[Annual sale]	Cost	Difference
1	Option 1 :	440	0	440
2	Option 2 :	640	200	440
3	Option 3 :	730	250	480

Ans. Option 3.

23. Expected profit from project 1 = \$3200
Expected profit from project 2 = \$2000   Gives more than 6% return.
Expected profit from project 3 = \$2400
Expected profit from project 4 = \$2200

Ans: project 1.2.3
Expected rate of return = .076.

24. Expected profit when the grocer buys 1 unit: 8¢
                                            2 units: 0.9 x (16) + 0.1(-4) = 14¢
                                            3 units: 0.1(8-2x4)+.15(16-4)+0.75(24)=

                                                                            19.8¢

   4 units: 0.1(8-3x4)+.15(16-2x4)+.25(24-4)+.5(32) = 21¢
   5 units: 0.1(8-4x4)+.15(16-3x4)+.25(24-8)+.25(32-4)+.25(40) = 20.8¢
   6 units: 0.1(8-5x4)+.15(16-4x4)+.25(24-3x4)+.25(32-2x4)+15(40-4)+.1(48)
              = 18¢
   7 units: 0.1(8-8x4)+.15(16-4x5)+.25(24-4x4)+25(32-3x4)+15(40-2x4)+.05(48-4)
              +.05(56) = 15.2¢

   Ans: 4 units.

25. $p \geq \dfrac{ML}{ML + MP} = \dfrac{4}{4 + 8} = 0.33$

    From the Poisson table

            p(demand $\geq$ 3) = 0.4633

            p(demand $\geq$ 4) = 0.2745

    Therefore   ans: 3 units.

26. $p \geq \dfrac{ML}{ML + MP} = \dfrac{43}{43 + 89} = .326$

    $\dfrac{x - 150}{12} = -.94$ (From normal p.d.f. table)

    x = 138.72

    ANS: 138.72

27. Expected profit when they charter
     15 buses   : 4200
     16 buses   : (4200-200)x .13 +(4480 x.87) = 4417.6
     17 buses   : (4200-2x200)x.13+(4480-200)x.17+(4760x.7) = 4553.6
     18 buses   : 4603.2
     19 buses   : 4528

    Ans: 18 buses profit = $4603.20

28. The probability that the movie can be shown for profit for.a
     maximum of eight weeks = .80
     The movie distributor's condition seems to be untenable based on a
     probability value of .80. [Note: This problem needs additional
     data for a better answer].

29. week

0	8				
1	1.2	1.2			
2	.2	.18	3.8		
3	3.6	.3	.57	4.47	
4	1.6	.48	.95	.6705	3.7005

Replacing all components once in

$$1 \text{ month costs } 55 + 1.2 \times 25 = 85/\text{month}$$
$$2 \text{ months costs } 55 + 3.38 \times 25 = 139.5/2 \text{ month} = 69.6/\text{month}$$
$$3 \text{ months costs } 55 + 9.47 \times 25 = 291.75/3 \text{ month} = 97.25/\text{month}$$
$$4 \text{ months costs } 55 + 13.1705 \times 25 = 384.2/4 \text{ month} = 96.05/\text{month}$$

Ans: Replace all components once in 2 months.

30. Month

0	150						
1	12	12					
2	25.5	.96	26.46				
3	49.5	2.04	2.12	53.66			
4	31.5	3.96	4.5	4.29	44.24		
5	22.5	2.52	8.73	9.12	3.54	46.41	
6	9	1.8	5.56	17.7	7.52	3.71	45.29

Replacing all tires once in

1 month	costs	285 ($/month)
2		208.65
3		228.5
4		226.7
5		227.7
7		227.5

Ans: Replace all tires once in 2 months.

Product Improvement Option	Advertising Strategy	1st Year Economic Condition	2nd Year Economic Condition	Net return

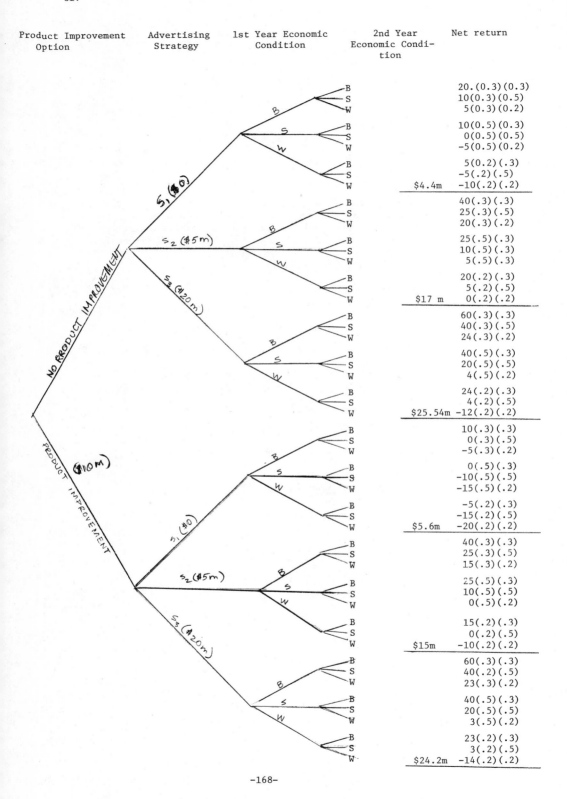

B   20.(0.3)(0.3)
S   10(0.3)(0.5)
W   5(0.3)(0.2)

B   10(0.5)(0.3)
S   0(0.5)(0.5)
W   −5(0.5)(0.2)

B   5(0.2)(.3)
S   −5(.2)(.5)
W $4.4m   −10(.2)(.2)

B   40(.3)(.3)
S   25(.3)(.5)
W   20(.3)(.2)

B   25(.5)(.3)
S   10(.5)(.3)
W   5(.5)(.3)

B   20(.2)(.3)
S   5(.2)(.5)
W $17 m   0(.2)(.2)

B   60(.3)(.3)
S   40(.3)(.5)
W   24(.3)(.2)

B   40(.5)(.3)
S   20(.5)(.5)
W   4(.5)(.2)

B   24(.2)(.3)
S   4(.2)(.5)
W $25.54m −12(.2)(.2)

B   10(.3)(.3)
S   0(.3)(.5)
W   −5(.3)(.2)

B   0(.5)(.3)
S   −10(.5)(.5)
W   −15(.5)(.2)

B   −5(.2)(.3)
S   −15(.2)(.5)
W $5.6m   −20(.2)(.2)

B   40(.3)(.3)
S   25(.3)(.5)
W   15(.3)(.2)

B   25(.5)(.3)
S   10(.5)(.5)
W   0(.5)(.2)

B   15(.2)(.3)
S   0(.2)(.5)
W $15m   −10(.2)(.2)

B   60(.3)(.3)
S   40(.2)(.5)
W   23(.3)(.2)

B   40(.5)(.3)
S   20(.5)(.5)
W   3(.5)(.2)

B   23(.2)(.3)
S   3(.2)(.5)
W $24.2m −14(.2)(.2)

$S_1(\$0)$

$S_2(\$5m)$

$S_3(\$20m)$

NO PRODUCT IMPROVEMENT

PRODUCT IMPROVEMENT $(\$10M)$

$S_1(\$0)$

$S_2(\$5m)$

$S_3(\$20m)$

32.	Toy	Annual Sales	Probability

	750,000	.3
	500,000	.35
	250,000	.35
	600,000	.55
	350,000	.25
	150,000	.20
	700,000	.40
	550,000	.35
	350,000	.25

A ($40,000)

B ($100,000)

C ($160,000)

33.

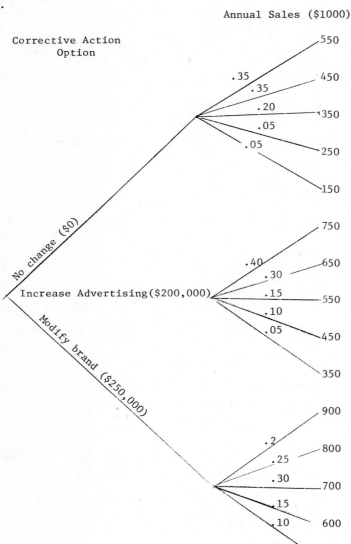

Annual Sales ($1000)

Corrective Action
Option

No change ($0)

Increase Advertising ($200,000)

Modify brand ($250,000)

.35   550

.35   450

.20   350

.05   250

.05   150

.40   750

.30   650

.15   550

.10   450

.05   350

.2   900

.25   800

.30   700

.15   600

.10   500

Chapter 11. Markov Models

1. $n_{00} = 4$ $n_{01} = 8$ $n_{10} = 8$ $n_{11} = 1$ $n_{12} = 16$ $n_{21} = 16$ $n_{22} = 21$

   $n_{02} = n_{20} = 0.$

$$\hat{p} = \begin{bmatrix} 4/12 & 8/12 & 0 \\ 8/25 & 1/25 & 16/25 \\ 0 & 16/37 & 21/37 \end{bmatrix}$$

using $\pi P = \pi$.

$\pi = (\pi_0, \pi_1, \pi_2) = (6/37, \ 25/74, \ 1/2)$

2. $n_{00} = 8$ $n_{01} = 12$ $n_{10} = 12$ $n_{11} = 17$

$$\hat{p} = \begin{bmatrix} 2/5 & 3/5 \\ 12/29 & 11/29 \end{bmatrix}$$

Using $\pi P = \pi$

$\pi = (\pi_0, \pi_1) = (60.147, \ 87/147)$

$\pi_1 = \Pr$ [a job waiting after a job completion in the long run] $= .591 < .85$

Answer: NO.

3. $n_{00} = 2$ $n_{01} = 6$ $n_{02} = 2$

   $n_{10} = 3$ $n_{11} = 5$ $n_{12} = 13$

   $n_{20} = 4$ $n_{21} = 7$ $n_{22} = 18$

$$\hat{p} = \begin{bmatrix} 1/5 & 3/5 & 1/5 \\ 3/21 & 51/21 & 13/21 \\ 4/29 & 7/29 & 18/29 \end{bmatrix} \quad , \quad \pi = [.148, \ .293, \ .558]$$

E[busy line] $= 0 \times .148 + 1 \times .293 + 2 \times .558 = 1.409.$

E[length of busy stretch] $= \dfrac{1}{\pi_0} = 6.76$ (of 2 min. interval)

About 56% of the customers will find all telephones busy.

4. Time intervals between call arrival epochs and holding times of calls are represented better by continuous random variables. A continuous time model is a better model.

5. Under present policy (π_A = market share for A, π_B = market share for B): $\pi_A = \pi_B = 1/2 \Rightarrow$ (eventual market share is same for A and B).

   With the new policy: $\pi_A = \pi_B = 1/2$

   The improvement shown is in smoothing out fluctuations and not in eventual market share.

6. Markov chain model is appropriate

   (i)   to represent the behavior of the consumer who has a habit of changing his brands often
   (ii) to measure the transient effect of advertising and
   (iii) to measure the overall market share.

   (a) consumer stays with the same brand; (b) Brand switching is cyclic, (c) no repeat buying; choice of remaining brands at random, (d) Eventual market share even; uniform buying behavior.

7. $\pi_{+1} = \dfrac{72}{147}$ $\pi_0 = \dfrac{45}{147}$ $\pi_{-1} = \dfrac{30}{147}$

   $\dfrac{1}{\pi_{-1}} = \dfrac{147}{30} = 4.9$ (yrs)

8. $\pi_0 = \dfrac{b}{a+b} = 0.7$ $\pi_1 = 1-\pi_0 = 0.3$

   (Here we assumed 100 is sufficiently big number of transitions to reach steady-state)

   True: 70
   False: 30

9.

$$\|P_{ij}\| = \begin{array}{c} \\ A \\ B \\ C \end{array} \begin{array}{ccc} A & B & C \\ .85 & .05 & .1 \\ .08 & .77 & .15 \\ .06 & .05 & .89 \end{array} \qquad p^2 = \begin{vmatrix} 0.7325 & .086 & 0.1815 \\ .1386 & .5994 & .2575 \\ .1084 & .086 & .8056 \end{vmatrix}$$

$$p^3 = \begin{vmatrix} .640 & .112 & .247 \\ .182 & .481 & .333 \\ 0.147 & .112 & .741 \end{vmatrix}$$

Market share

		A	B	C
July:	$(.5, .2, .3)$ $P =$	$(.459,$	$.194,$	$.347)$
Aug:	$(.5, .2, .3)$ $P^2 =$	$(.426,$	$.188,$	$.387)$
Sept:	$(.5, 12, 13)$ $P^3 =$	$(.4,$	$.186$	$.414)$

Ultimate $= (\pi_A, \pi_B, \pi_C)$
Market share $= (.294, .1, .615)$

10. $\pi_A = .905$

$\pi_s = .06$

$\pi_u = .035$

\#(Acceptable) = 1357.5
\#(seconds)   =   90
\#(Unacceptable) = 52.5

11.

	S	U
S	.7	.3
U	.9	.1

$\pi_s = .75$

$\pi_u = .25$

under new policy

	S	U
S	.7	.3
U	.99	.01

$\pi_s = .77$

$\pi_s = .23$

To make $\pi_s \geq .9$; increase P_{ss} such that

$$x \, \pi_s + .99\pi_u = \pi_s \Rightarrow .99\pi_u = (1-x)\pi_s$$

$$\pi_s = \frac{.99}{(1-x)} \pi_u \qquad \pi_s + \pi_0 = 1$$

$$\Rightarrow \pi_u = \frac{1-x}{1.99-x} \leq 0.9 \quad \Rightarrow P_{ss} = x \geq 0.89.$$

12. $\pi_A = .35$ $\pi_B = .54$ $\pi_C = .11$

Existing market share: $(.22, .57, .21)$
The policy satisfies company objectives.

13. Assume replacements take place at the end of every week.

Define

$P_{ij} = P_r$ [i week(s) old component at the end of certain week become j week(s) old one at the end of next week]

$$
\| P_{ij} \| =
\begin{array}{c c}
 & \begin{array}{cccc} 0 & 1 & 2 & 3 \end{array} \\
\begin{array}{c} 0 \\ 1 \\ 2 \\ 3 \end{array} &
\left[
\begin{array}{cccc}
.15 & .85 & 0 & 0 \\
.353 & 0 & .647 & 0 \\
.636 & 0 & 0 & .364 \\
1 & 0 & 0 &
\end{array}
\right]
\end{array}
$$

where P_{12} and P_{23} are obtained as follows.

$P_{12} = P_r$ [component not replaced at the end of 2nd week/component not replaced at the end of 1st week]

$$= \frac{0.55}{0.85} = .647.$$

$\pi_0 = .38 \qquad \pi_1 = .33 \qquad \pi_2 = .21 \qquad \pi_3 = .08$

Long run age distribution:

```
#(New)          . = 38%
#(1 week old)     = 33%
#(2 week old)     = 21%
#(3 week old)     =  8%.
```

14. $\pi_1 = .20 \quad \pi_2 = .35 \quad \pi_3 = 0.17 \quad \pi_4 = 0.28$

Ans: a) location 2. b) location 3 since $P_{23} > P_{21}, P_{22}, P_{24}$

15.

$$
\| P_{ij} \| =
\begin{array}{c c}
 & \begin{array}{ccccc} 0 & 1 & 2 & B & p \end{array} \\
\begin{array}{c} 0 \\ 1 \\ 2 \\ B \\ P \end{array} &
\left[
\begin{array}{ccccc}
0.694 & .300 & 0 & 0 & 0.006 \\
0.438 & .326 & 0.224 & 0 & 0.012 \\
0.244 & .308 & .374 & .052 & .022 \\
0 & 0 & 0 & 1 & 0 \\
0 & 0 & 0 & 0 & 1
\end{array}
\right]
\end{array}
$$

Use: $P^{12} = P^8 P^4$

$$P^8 = P^4 P^4, \quad P^4 = P^2 P^2.$$

$$P^{12} = P^4 \times P^8 = \begin{bmatrix} .555 & .302 & .104 & .009 & .030 \\ .501 & .283 & .103 & .022 & .098 \\ .472 & .273 & .114 & .088 & .053 \\ 0 & 0 & 0 & 1 & 0 \\ 0 & 0 & 0 & 0 & 1 \end{bmatrix} \begin{bmatrix} .500 & .261 & .080 & .079 & .08 \\ .455 & .254 & .082 & .085 & .124 \\ .450 & .253 & .09 & .107 & .1 \\ 0 & 0 & 0 & 1 & 0 \\ 0 & 0 & 0 & 0 & 1 \end{bmatrix}$$

$$= \begin{bmatrix} .462 & .248 & .078 & .092 & .120 \\ .423 & .226 & .072 & .096 & .183 \\ 0.412 & .221 & .070 & .160 & .137 \\ 0 & 0 & 0 & 1 & 0 \\ 0 & 0 & 0 & 0 & 1 \end{bmatrix}$$

$$[432, 345, 230] \times \begin{bmatrix} .462 & .248 & .078 & .092 & .120 \\ .423 & .226 & .072 & .096 & .183 \\ .412 & .221 & .070 & 0.160 & .137 \end{bmatrix} =$$

$$\begin{array}{ccccc} 0 & 1 & 2 & B & P \\ = [\quad 440 & 235 & 76 & 110 & 146 \ ] \end{array}$$

Expected loss = 110 x 63 = 6930 ($)

16.

$$P = \begin{array}{c} \\ 1 \\ 3 \\ 0 \\ 2 \end{array} \begin{array}{cccc} 1 & 3 & 0 & 2 \\ \begin{bmatrix} 1 & 0 & 0 & 0 \\ 0 & 1 & 0 & 0 \\ 0.095 & 0 & 0.379 & 0.526 \\ 0 & .154 & .409 & .437 \end{bmatrix} \end{array}$$

$$P^2 = \begin{bmatrix} 1 & 0 & 0 & 0 \\ 0 & 1 & 0 & 0 \\ .131 & .082 & .358 & .429 \\ .039 & .221 & .334 & .406 \end{bmatrix}$$

$$P^4 = \begin{array}{c} \\ 1 \\ 3 \\ 0 \\ 2 \end{array} \begin{array}{cccc} 1 & 3 & 0 & 2 \\ \begin{bmatrix} 1 & 0 & 0 & 0 \\ 0 & 1 & 0 & 0 \\ .194 & .206 & .272 & .328 \\ .098 & .338 & .255 & .309 \end{bmatrix} \end{array}$$

P_r [patient survives longer than four observations]

$$= P_{00}^{(4)} + P_{02}^{(4)} = .522$$

P_r [John will die within the next two observations] $= P_{21}^{(2)} + P_{23}^{(2)} = .26$

17. Transpose of the transition probability matrix also has the properties of a transition probability matrix. Therefore both rows and columns of π should have identical elements.

20.

	F	S	J	SE	D
F	.05	.85	0	0	.1
S	0	.03	.92	0	.05
J	0	0	.02	.95	.03
SE	0	0	0	.99	.01
D	0	0	0	0	1

$p =$

$p^4 =$

	F	S	J	SE	D
F	0.	.0004	.0530	.8469	.1834
S	0	0	·0	.9015	.0985
J	0	0	.0	.9407	.0593
SE	0	0	·0	.9605	.0395
D	0	0	0	0	1

.0 very small number

Ans: 18.34%

21. Estimate the number of graduates added to the work force in each category using appropriate transition probability matrix P, P^2, P^3 or P^4.

22. P_r [both hit] $= 2/5 \times 8/3 = 4/15$ $= P(AB \rightarrow E)$

P [A hit B, B fail] $= 2/5 \times (1 - 2/3) = 2/15$ $= P(AB \rightarrow A)$
P [B hit A, A fail] $= (1 - 2/5)(2/3) = 6/15$ $= P(AB \rightarrow B)$
P [A fail, B fail] $= (L - 2/5)(1 - 2/3) = 3/15$ $= P(AB \rightarrow AB)$

23. No. of toasters constructs the state space.

$$\begin{array}{c c c c c c c} & 3 & 4 & 5 & 6 & 7 & 8 \\ 3 & .1 & 0 & 0 & 0 & 0 & .9 \\ 4 & .2 & .1 & 0 & 0 & 0 & .7 \\ 5 & .4 & .2 & .1 & 0 & 0 & .3 \\ 6 & .3 & .4 & .2 & .1 & 0 & 0 \\ 7 & 0 & .3 & .4 & .2 & .1 & 0 \\ 8 & 0 & 0 & .3 & .4 & .2 & .1 \end{array}$$

24. Identify the number of movers. Use long run probability distribution to indicate the industry where a mover can be found.

25. Let the state space be the number of successive defective radios, then

$$P_{ij} = \begin{array}{c c c c} & 0 & 1 & 2 \\ 0 & .99 & .01 & 0 \\ 1 & .99 & 0 & .01 \\ 2 & 0 & 0 & 1 \end{array}$$

P_{22} is the absorbing state since once number of successive defective radios reaches 2 the inspection stops. Probability the lot is accepted $= 1 - P_{02}^{(100)}$ where $P_{02}^{(100)}$ is the $(0,2)$ element of P^{100}.

26.

$$\begin{array}{c c c c c c c} & 0 & 1 & 2 & 3 & 4 & 5 \\ 0 & .999 & .001 & & & & \\ 1 & .999 & 0 & .001 & & & \\ 2 & .999 & 0 & 0 & .001 & & \\ 3 & .999 & 0 & 0 & 0 & .001 & \\ 4 & .999 & 0 & 0 & 0 & 0 & .001 \\ 5 & 0 & 0 & 0 & 0 & 0 & 1 \end{array}$$

Reliability of the structure = Probability that the structure does not fail
$$= 1 = P_{05}^{(10,000)}$$

where $P_{05}^{(10,000)}$ is the $(0,5)$ element of $P^{10,000}$.

1. $40/42 = 20/21$ (Hr.)

2. $\sum_{i=3}^{5} \binom{5}{i} (\frac{20}{21})^i (\frac{1}{21})^{5-i} = .9989$

3. P[a certain repairman is busy] $= 45/65 = 9/13$

    Average number of busy repairman $= \sum_{i=1}^{8} i \binom{8}{i} (\frac{9}{13})^i (\frac{4}{13})^{8-i}$

    $= 5.93$ (mean of binomial distribution $= np$)

    P[at least one repairman available]

    $= 1 - P[\text{No repairman available}] = 1 - \binom{8}{0} (\frac{9}{13})^0 (\frac{4}{13})^i = 0.9999.$

4. (Assume exponential arrival and service time)

    M/M/s/s : s=4

    Rush hour: $\rho=8$

    $P_4 = (8^4/4!)/(1+8+8^2/2!+8^3/3!+8^4/4!) = .5746$ (= 57.46%)

    Normal hour $\rho=2$

    $P_4 = (2^4/4!)/(1+2+2^2/2!+2^3/3!+2^4/4!) = .0952$ (= 9.52%)

    By increasing the arrival rate 0.5/min → 2/min (4 times)

    the percentage of blocking increased 9.52% → 57.46% (6 times)

5. case 1; original system (2 groups)

    $$\rho = \frac{.5}{0.5} = 1.0$$

    $$P_s = \frac{\frac{(10)^3}{3!}}{1+10+10^2/2!+(10^3)/3!} = .7320$$

    case 2: Pooled system.

$$P_s = \frac{\dfrac{(20)^3}{6!}}{j+ \displaystyle\sum_{i=1}^{6} \frac{(20)^i}{i!}} \approx .7181 \qquad \rho = 20$$

Since P_s is the Probability of blocking the lines "pooling all six lines" case is preferable.

6. M/M/∞ : $\rho = \dfrac{0.5}{0.1} = 5$

    E[number of customers in the system] $= \displaystyle\sum_{n=1}^{\infty} nP_n = \sum_{n=1}^{\infty} ne^{-5}\frac{5^n}{n!}$

    $= 5 \displaystyle\sum_{n=1}^{\infty} \frac{e^{-5} 5^{n-1}}{(n-1)!} = 5 \sum_{n=0}^{\infty} \frac{e^{-5} 5^n}{n!} = 5e^{-5} \cdot e^5 = 5$

    [Note: The Mean of a Poisson distribution with parameter p is p].

7. M/M/1 : $\rho = 3/4$

    $P_0 = 1 - \rho = 1/4.$

    E[length of time the runway is used in a given hour] $= 1 \times (1-P_0) = 3/4$ hr.

    E[waiting time in the queue] $= E[W]$

    $= \dfrac{\lambda}{\mu(\mu-\lambda)} = \dfrac{15}{20(20-15)} = 3/20$ (hr.)

8. M/M/1 : $\rho = 4/5$

    $E[W + S] = \dfrac{1}{\mu-\lambda} = 1$ (hr.)

    E[doctor's free time] $= P_0 \times 6 = (1 - 4/5)6 = 6/5$ (hr.)

9. M/M/1 : $\rho = 2/3$

    $P_0 = (1 - \rho) = 1/3.$

10. M/M/1 : $E[W] = \dfrac{\lambda}{\mu(\mu-\lambda)} = \dfrac{20}{\mu(\mu-20)} \leq 5$

    average service rate ≥ 30 (customers/hr)

11. M/M/2 : $\rho = \dfrac{\lambda}{s\mu} = 3/4$

a) $P_0 = [\sum_{r=0}^{2} (\dfrac{2 \times 3/4}{r!})^r + \dfrac{(3/4)^3 2^2}{2!(1-3/4)}]^{-1} = 1/7$

$P_1 = [2 \times 3/4] P_0 = 3/14$

Prob of waiting for service $= 1 = P_0 - P_1 = 9/14$

b) Expected percentage of idle time for each clerk =

$= (1 - \rho) \times 100$

$= 25\%$

Also $= (P_0 + 1/2\ P_1) 100.$

$= 25\%.$

12. M/M/2: $\rho = 5/6$

$P_0 = [\sum_{r=0}^{2} (\dfrac{2 \times 5/6}{r!})^r + \dfrac{(5/6)^3 2^2}{2!(1-5/6)}]^{-1} = 36/371$

$P_s = \dfrac{4 \times 25/36}{2!} \times \dfrac{36}{371} = 50/371$

$E[W] = \dfrac{50/371}{24 \times 1/36} = 75/371$ (hr.)

13. M/M/1 : $\rho = 5/6$

$E[W] = \dfrac{20}{24 \times 4} = 5/24$

Waiting time in the queue will be increased by $[\dfrac{5}{24} - \dfrac{75}{371}] = .006$ hr.

14. M/M/1 : $\rho = 2/3$

$E[W + S] = \dfrac{1}{\mu-\lambda} = \dfrac{1}{12-8} \times 8 = 2$ (hrs.)

15. When $\rho = 2/3$ $P_0 = 1 - \rho = 1/3$

now $\rho = \dfrac{9.6}{12}$ $P_0 = 1 - \dfrac{9.6}{12} = 1/5$

Idle time reduction $= (1/3 - 1/5) 8 = 16/15$ hours per day

waiting line increased by: $E[N_2^1] - E[N_1^1] = \lambda_2 E[W_2^1] - \lambda_1 E[W_4]$

$= \lambda_2 (\dfrac{\lambda_2}{\mu(\mu-\lambda_2)}) - \lambda_1 (\dfrac{\lambda_1}{\mu(\mu-\lambda_1)}) = 1.89$

where $\lambda_1 = 8$, $\lambda_2 = 9.6$

Total time spent in System is increased by:

$$\frac{1}{\mu-\lambda_2} - \frac{1}{\mu-\lambda_1} = \frac{1}{12 - 9.6} - \frac{1}{12 - 8} = .1667 \text{ day}$$
$$= \underline{1.333 \text{ hrs.}}$$

16. When input rate is 1/hr.

E[N] = 2.

E[Profit] = E[income] - E[expenditure]

= E[number of repaired car] x 20 - 8 x 10 - E[N]C

= 80 - 2c

when input rate is 1.2/hr., E[N] = 3.89

E[Profit] = 9.6 x 20 - 8 x 10 - 3.89 C = 112 - 3.89 C

One car per hour is preferred over 1.2 cars per hour if

$80 - 2C \geq 112 - 3.89 C$ $\underline{C \geq 16.93}$

17. An assignment of 12 cars per day would make p = 1
in the model and in practice would result in overtime work by
the mechanic.

18. M/M/1: David: ρ = 1/2

E[N] = 1/2

cost: 15 + 2.5 = 17.5 $/hr.

George: ρ = 2/3

E[N] = 1

cost: 12 + 5 = 17 $/hr.

19. M/M/1: 1. Without new equipment

$E[N] = \frac{\rho}{1-\rho} = 7/3$

E[Cost incurred] = 7.3 x 5 = $ 35/3 min.

2. With new equipment

$E[N] = \frac{1/2}{1/2} = 1$

E[Cost incurred] = 1 x 5 + 10 = $15 min., therefore, do not purchase
the new equipment.

20. M/M/1/3: $\rho = 3/4$.

$$P_3 = \frac{1-3/4}{1-(3/4)^4} (3/4)^3 = .1543.$$

$$P_3 \times P_3 = .023.$$

21. M/M/1/3: $P_1 = 3/2\, P_0 \quad P_2 = (3/2)^2 P_0 \quad P_3 = (3/2)^3 P_0 \Rightarrow P_0 = .1230$

$$P_3 = .4151$$

$$P_3 \times P_3 = .1723.$$

(Note: since $\rho > 1$ the formulas in P_0 316 does hold any more)

22. M/D/1/3:

  ① arrival rate during each 15 min: 3/4 (man/15 min.)

  ②. arrival rate during each 15 min: 3/2 (man/15 min.)

①.

	0	1	2	3
0	0.472	0.3542	.13285	.04095
1	0.472	0.3542	.13285	.04095
2		0.472	0.3542	.1738
3			.472	.528

$\pi_0 = .2344 \qquad \pi_1 = .2623 \qquad \pi_2 = .2922 \qquad \pi_3 = .2111$

P[System full] $= \pi_3 = .2111$

②.

	0	1	2	3
0	.2231	.3347	.2510	.1912
1	.2231	.3347	.2510	.1912
2		.2231	.3347	.4422
3			.2231	.7769

$\pi_0 = .1287 \qquad \pi_1 = 3.482\pi_0 \qquad \pi_2 = 8.883\pi_0 \qquad \pi_3 = 21.44\pi_0$

P[System full] $= \pi_3 = .6153.$

1. If shortages are <u>allowed</u>, then there is the option of incurring shortages or not. If no shortages are allowed, then there are few options. Thus allowing shortages cannot increase the cost.

2.

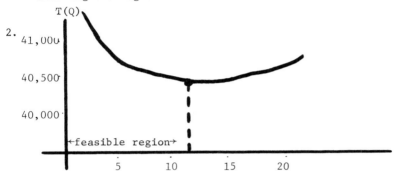

The optimum ordering level is Q* = 10.
An order is placed every Q*/50 = .2 month.

3(a) The holding cost and penalty cost for each product class is tabulated below:

PRODUCT COST	HOLDING COST	PENALTY COST
1	$1.25	$500
2	2.19	700
3	0.38	250
4	0.88	200

3(b)

PRODUCT CLASS	$\bar{Q}* = \sqrt{2r\,C/h}\ \sqrt{(p+h)/p}$	$t* = \bar{Q}*/r = \sqrt{2C/hr}\ \sqrt{(p+h)/p}$
1	40.05	2.002
2	42.80	1.070
3	51.34	5.134
4	41.38	2.758

3(c)

PRODUCT CLASS	$Q^* = \sqrt{2rC/h}$	$t^* = Q^*/r = \sqrt{2C/rh}$ months
1	40.00	2.000
2	42.74	1.068
3	51.30	5.130
4	41.29	2.752

NOTE: The results in part (b) and (c) are nearly the same because the factor $(p+h)/p \approx 1$.

4(a) The holding cost and penalty cost for each product class is tabulated below:

PRODUCT CLASS	HOLDING COST	PENALTY COST
1	$1.38	$300
2	2.41	350
3	0.41	190
4	0.96	60

4(b)

PRODUCT CLASS	$\bar{Q}^* = \sqrt{2rC/h}\sqrt{(p+h)/p}$	$t^* = \bar{Q}^*/r = \sqrt{2C/rh}\sqrt{(p+h)/p}$
1	48.26	2.413
2	51.71	1.293
3	62.54	6.254
4	50.40	3.360

4(c)

PRODUCT CLASS	$Q^* = \sqrt{2rC/h}$ units	$t^* = Q^*/r = \sqrt{2C/rh}$ months
1	48.15	2.408
2	51.53	1.288
3	62.47	6.247
4	50.00	3.333

5.

	SUPPLY POINTS			DEMAND POINTS		

SUPPLY POINTS

DEMAND POINTS

Chicago
- ① Winter
- ② Spring
- ③ Summer
- ④ Fall

Winter ①
Spring ②
Summer ③
Fall ④

Warehouse **1**

Winter ⑤
Spring ⑥
Summer ⑦
Fall ⑧

Warehouse **2**

Pittsburgh
- ⑤ Winter
- ⑥ Spring
- ⑦ Summer
- ⑧ Summer

Winter ⑨
Spring ⑩
Summer ⑪
Fall ⑫

Warehouse **3**

5 (cont.)

Objective Function Coefficients

		Warehouse 1				Warehouse 2				Warehouse 3			
		W	Sp.	Su.	F	W	Sp.	Su.	F	W	Sp.	Su.	F
Supply Points		1	2	3	4	5	6	7	8	9	10	11	12
	W 1	108	113	118	123	106	111	116	121	109	114	119	124
	Sp. 2	∞	108	113	118	∞	106	111	116	∞	109	114	119
Chicago	Su. 3	∞	∞	108	113	∞	∞	106	111	∞	∞	109	114
	F 4	∞	∞	∞	108	∞	∞	∞	106	∞	∞	∞	109
	W 5	104	110	116	122	98	104	110	116	100	106	112	118
	Sp. 6	∞	104	110	116	∞	98	104	110	∞	100	106	112
Pittsburgh	Su. 7	∞	∞	104	110	∞	∞	98	104	∞	∞	100	106
	F 8	∞	∞	∞	104	∞	∞	∞	98	∞	∞	∞	100

Let x_{ij} = number of units sent from supply point i to demand point j where

i=1, 2,...,8   and   j=1, 2,...,12.

Supply Constraints

$$\sum_{j=1}^{12} x_{ij} \le 2,500 \qquad i=1, 2, 3, 4$$

$$\sum_{j=1}^{12} x_{ij} \le 5,000 \qquad i=5, 6, 7, 8$$

Demand Constraints

$$\sum_{i=1}^{8} x_{i1} = 1,200$$

$$\sum_{i=1}^{8} x_{i2} = 4,000$$

$$\sum_{i=1}^{8} x_{i3} = 5,000$$

5 continued

$$\sum_{i=1}^{8} x_{i4} = 1,000$$

$$\sum_{i=1}^{8} x_{i5} = 1,000$$

$$\sum_{i=1}^{8} x_{i6} = 3,000$$

$$\sum_{i=1}^{8} x_{i7} = 3,500$$

$$\sum_{i=1}^{8} x_{i8} = 800$$

$$\sum_{i=1}^{8} x_{i9} = 1,300$$

$$\sum_{i=1}^{8} x_{i10} = 3,500$$

$$\sum_{i=1}^{8} x_{i11} = 4,000$$

$$\sum_{i=1}^{8} x_{i12} = 900$$

$$x_{ij} = 0, 1, 2,... \qquad i=1, 2,...8; \; j=1, 2,...,12$$

6. Let number of periods in a cycle = k
    Let number of factories = n
    Let number of retail distributors = m

    Then, number of nodes = $k(n+m)$
          number of arcs = $(kn)(km) = k^2 nm$

    In the given problem:

    k=24, n=5, m=150

    Therefore, number of nodes = $24(5+150) = 3,720$
              number of arcs = $(24)(24)(5)(150) = 432,000$

7.

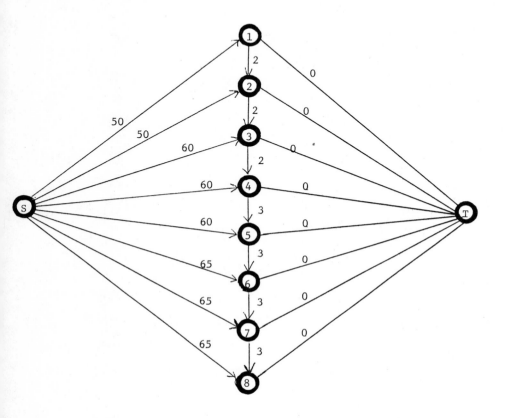

Inventory Network with "Shipping" Costs for each Arc

7 continued

NODE	SHORTEST PATH FROM SOURCE
<u>1</u>	5→1
<u>2</u>	5→2
<u>3</u>	5→2→3
<u>4</u>	5→2→3→4
<u>5</u>	5→2→3→4→5
<u>6</u>	5→2→3→4→5→6
<u>7</u>	5→2→3→4→5→6→7
<u>8</u>	5→8

MONTH	OPTIMUM PRODUCTION	OPTIMUM STORAGE
<u>1</u>	100	0
<u>2</u>	75 + 60 + 80 + 110 + 130 + 100 = 555	(555 − 75) = 480
<u>3</u>	0	(480 − 60) = 420
<u>4</u>	0	(420 − 80) = 340
<u>5</u>	0	(340 − 110) = 230
<u>6</u>	0	(230 − 130) = 100
<u>7</u>	0	(100 − 100) = 0
<u>8</u>	75	0

<u>Optimum Production & Storage Levels In Each Month</u>

8. The shortest path changes only for node 8 to $5 \rightarrow 2 \rightarrow 3 \rightarrow 4 \rightarrow 5 \rightarrow 6 \rightarrow 7 \rightarrow 8$.

The optimum production and storage levels in each month are:

MONTH	OPTIMUM PRODUCTION	OPTIMUM STORAGE
1	100	0
2	75 + 60 + 80 + 110 + 130 + 100 + 75 = 630	(630 − 75) = 555
3	0	(555 − 60) = 495
4	0	(495 − 80) = 415
5	0	(415 − 110) = 305
6	0	(305 − 130) = 175
7	0	(175 − 100) = 75
8	0	(75 − 75) = 0

9(a) Let x_j = regular time production in month j, j=1, 2, 3, 4, 5, 6

y_j = overtime production in month j, j=1, 2, 3, 4, 5, 6

s_j = amount in storage in month j, j=1, 2, 3, 4, 5

Constraints (Demand)

$$x_1 + y_1 - s_1 = 80$$

$$x_2 + y_2 + s_1 - s_2 = 70$$

$$x_3 + y_3 + s_2 - s_3 = 80$$

$$x_4 + y_4 + s_3 - s_4 = 90$$

$$x_5 + y_5 + s_4 - s_5 = 50$$

$$x_6 + y_6 + s_5 = 100$$

Storage Capacity Constraints

$$s_1 \leq 150$$

$$s_2 \leq 150$$

$$s_3 \leq 150$$

-190-

9(a), continued

<u>Storage Capacity Constraints</u> (cont.)

$$s_4 \leq 300$$

$$s_5 \leq 300$$

$$s_6 \leq 300$$

<u>Production Capacity Constraints</u>

$x_j \leq 60$	j=1, 2, 3, 4
$x_j \leq 80$	j=5, 6
$y_j \leq 15$	j=1, 2, 3, 4
$y_j \leq 20$	j=5, 6

<u>Non-Negativity Constraints</u>

$$x_j, \; y_j, \; s_j \geq 0 \qquad\qquad j=1, 2, 3, 4, 5, 6$$

<u>OBJECTIVE FUNCTION</u>

MINIMIZE: $10(x_1 + x_2) + 12(x_3 + x_4 + x_5) + 15(x_6)$

$\qquad + 13(y_1 + y_2) + 15.6 \; (y_3 + y_4 + y_5) + 19.5(y_6)$

$\qquad + 1(s_1 + s_2 + s_3 + s_4) + 2(s_5 + s_6)$

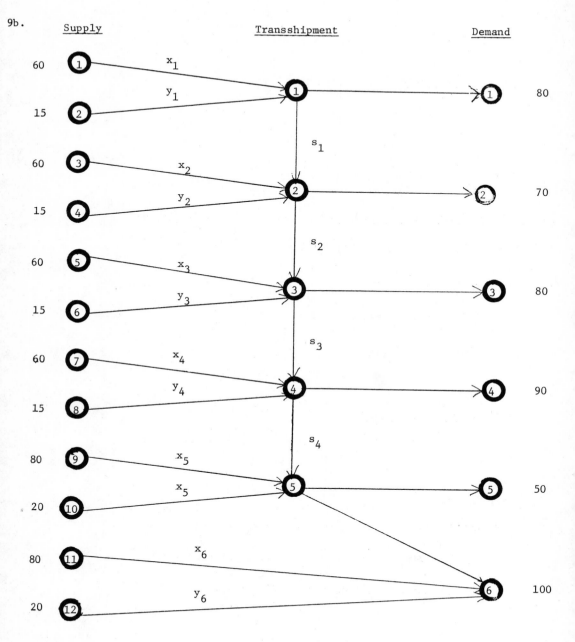

For each transshipment node, i, we place the storage capacity on arc (i, i + 1).

10. For the old machine,

$$\overline{Q}* = \sqrt{2(400)(500)/.5} \quad \sqrt{(25+.5)/25} \quad = 903.33$$

$$Q* = \sqrt{2(400)(500)/.5} \quad \sqrt{25/(25.5)} \quad = 885.61$$

Average cost is

$$[Cr/\overline{Q} + cr] + hQ^2/2\overline{Q} + p(\overline{Q}-Q)^2/2Q = 4442.80$$

This is the cost in each period of length $\overline{Q}/r = 2.258$ months. Thus, the annual cost is

$$4442.80(12/2.258) = 23,610.98$$

For the new machine,

$$\overline{Q}* = \sqrt{2(400)(200)/.5} \quad \sqrt{(15+.5)/15} \quad = 575.04$$

$$Q* = \sqrt{2(400)(200)/.5} \quad \sqrt{15/(15+.5)} \quad = 556.49$$

Average cost per cycle is 2278.24.

Since a cycle has length $\overline{Q}/r = 1.438$ months, the annual cost is

$$2278.24(12/1.438) + 15000 = 34011.74 \quad \text{(the 15000 is the annual rental)}$$

Thus the new equipment should not be rented.

11(a)

$$N = \frac{p-c}{p+h} = \frac{80-57}{80+0.1} = 0.287$$

Using (s,S) Formula #1,

$$P_{50} = 0.2 \not\geq 0.287 \text{ so } S \neq 50$$

$$P_{50} + P_{60} = 0.2 + 0.5 = 0.7 \geq 0.287 \text{ so } S = 60$$

Therefore, whenever an order is placed, the resulting inventory should be 60 units.

11(b) Use (s,S) Formula #2 to compute the value of s. The right hand side
of (30) is first computed as:

$10 + 57(60) + 0.1[(60-50)(0.2) + (60-60)(0.5)] + 80[(70-60)(0.3)] = 3670.2$

For s=50, the left hand side of (30) is:

$0.1(50-50)(0.2) + 80[(60-50)(0.5) + (70-50)(0.3)] + (57)(50) = 3730$

Thus s is not equal to 50. Since (30) holds for s=S, we have that
the smallest integer for which (30) holds is s=60. Therefore, whenever
the inventory drops below 60 units, it should be replenished up to 60
units.

12(a)

$$N = \frac{p-c}{p+h} = \frac{80-40}{80+0.1} = 0.499$$

Using (s,S) Formula #1,

$P_{50} = 0.2 \not\geq 0.499$ so $S \neq 50$

$P_{50} + P_{60} = 0.2 + 0.5 = 0.7 \geq 0.499$ so $S = 60$

Therefore, whenever an order is placed, the resulting inventory
should be 60 units.

12(b) Use (s,S) Formula #2 to compute the values of s.

The right hand side of (30) is first computed as:

$10 + 40(60) + 0.1[(60-50)(0.2) + (60-60)(0.5)] + 80[(70-60)(0.3)] = 2650.2$

For s=50, the left hand side of (30) is:

$0.1(50-50)(0.2) + 80[(60-50)(0.5) + (70-50)(0.3)] + (40)(50) = 2880$

Since 2880 > 2650.2, s is not equal to 50. Since (30) holds for s=S,
we have that the smallest integer for which (30) holds is s=60. Therefore,
whenever the inventory drops below 60 units, it should be replenished up
to 60 units.

13(a)

Revenue is	.30(800,000)	with probability .1
	.30(900,000)	with probability .2
	.30(1,000,000)	with probability .3
	.30(1,000,000)	with probability .3
	.30(1,000,000)	with probability .1

Thus E[Revenue] = .30(800,000)(.1) + .30(900,000)(.2) + .30(1,000,000)(.7)
                = $288,000

E[Profit] = E[Revenue] - cost
          = 288,000 - (1,000,000)(.08)
          = 288,000 - 80,000 = $208,000

13(b)

$$E[profit] = .30 \sum_{i \leq x} iP[X=i] + .30 \sum_{i > x} xP[X=x] - .08x$$

13(c)

p = .30   c = .08   C = 0   h = 0

N = (.30-.08)/(.30 + 0) = .733

Thus, S = 1,100,000 (s is not applicable).

14.

p = .35   c = .08   h = 0, so

N = (.35-.08)/(.35 + 0) = .771

Thus S=1,110,000

15.

N = (15-7)/(15 + .5) = .516
Thus S=150

16.

N = (15-7)/(15+1) = .50
Thus s=150

17.

1040 trees

18.

x_{it} = amount purchased under option i at beginning of month t

y_{it} = 1 option i selected at beginning of month t
       0 if not

I_t = inventory on hand at end of month t.

$$\text{MIN} \sum_{t=1}^{6} [10X_{1t} + 9.5X_{2t} + 9X_{3t} + 8X_{4t}] + 3I_1 + 3I_2 + 3I_3 + 4I_4 + 4I_5 + 4I_6$$

st $\quad \sum_{i=1}^{4} y_{it} \leq 1 \qquad t=1,\ldots,6$ (select <u>at most</u> 1 option each month)

$$1y_{1t} \leq x_{1t} \leq 100y_{1t}$$

$$101y_{2t} \leq x_{2t} \leq 500y_{2t}$$

amount purchased under
each option must lie
within option limits

$$501y_{3t} \leq x_{3t} \leq 1000y_{3t}$$

$$1001y_{4t} \leq x_{4t} \leq 3350y_{4t} \quad \text{(observe 3350 is the total demand)}$$

(Observe if $y_{it} = 1$, then $y_{jt} = 0$ all $j \neq i$)

$$\sum_{i=1}^{4} x_{i1} = 500 + I_1$$

$$I_1 + \sum_{i=1}^{4} x_{i2} = 600 + I_2$$

$$I_2 + \sum_{i=1}^{4} x_{i3} = 700 + I_3$$

$$I_3 + \sum_{i=1}^{4} x_{i4} = 450 + I_4$$

$$I_4 + \sum_{i=1}^{4} x_{i5} = 500 + I_5$$

$$I_5 + \sum_{i=1}^{4} x_{i6} = 600 + I_6$$

$$I_t \geq 0, \ x_{it} \geq 0, \ y_{it} = 0 \text{ or } 1$$